ECTIONS FOR HIGHER EDUCATION

Martin Kramer
EDITOR-IN-CHIEF

Total Quality Management on Campus: Is It Worth Doing?

Daniel Seymour
QSystems

EDITOR

Number 86, Summer 1994

JOSSEY-BASS PUBLISHERS
San Francisco

TOTAL QUALITY MANAGEMENT ON CAMPUS: IS IT WORTH DOING?
Daniel Seymour (ed.)
New Directions for Higher Education, no. 86
Volume XXII, Number 2
Martin Kramer, Editor-in-Chief

Microfilm copies of issues and articles are available in 16mm and 35mm, as well as microfiche in 105mm, through University Microfilms Inc., 300 North Zeeb Road, Ann Arbor, Michigan 48106-1346.

LC 85-644752 ISSN 0271-0560 ISBN 0-7879-9962-8

NEW DIRECTIONS FOR HIGHER EDUCATION is part of The Jossey-Bass Higher and Adult Education Series and is published quarterly by Jossey-Bass Inc., Publishers, 350 Sansome Street, San Francisco, California 94104-1342 (publication number USPS 990-880). Second-class postage paid at San Francisco, California, and at additional mailing offices. POSTMASTER: Send address changes to New Directions for Higher Education, Jossey-Bass Inc., Publishers, 350 Sansome Street, San Francisco, California 94104-1342.

SUBSCRIPTIONS for 1994 cost $47.00 for individuals and $62.00 for institutions, agencies, and libraries.

EDITORIAL CORRESPONDENCE should be sent to the Editor-in-Chief, Martin Kramer, 2807 Shasta Road, Berkeley, California 94708-2011.

Cover photograph and random dot by Richard Blair/Color & Light © 1990.

Manufactured in the United States of America. Nearly all Jossey-Bass books, jackets, and periodicals are printed on recycled paper that contains at least 50 percent recycled waste, including 10 percent postconsumer waste. Many of our materials are also printed with vegetable-based inks; during the printing process these inks emit fewer volatile organic compounds (VOCs) than petroleum-based inks. VOCs contribute to the formation of smog.

CONTENTS

EDITOR'S NOTES

Beginning in the late 1980s, a small number of colleges and universities decided to see whether the industry-based principles of total quality management (TQM) could help their institutions to respond to the challenges facing them. Those hopeful pioneers forged the way for a mass of interested followers, and TQM-related activities have surged. For example, the American Association for Higher Education (AAHE) held its first Assessment and Quality Conference in 1993. Many other organizations—including the American Assembly of Schools and Colleges of Business, the National Association of Schools of Public Affairs and Administration, and the League for Innovation in the Community College—have held standing-room-only workshops and sessions on quality management. Two of higher education's most prestigious journals, *Educational Record* and *Change,* have devoted entire issues to the subject ("Special Focus," 1993; "TQM," 1993).

A number of surveys have shed light on adoption rates and use patterns. Horine, Hailey, and Rubach (1993) report a study of higher education institutions in which more than 180 colleges, universities, and community colleges stated that they were implementing quality practices in administration. Many of the schools were also offering TQM-related courses. The American Council on Education's annual survey (El-Khawas, 1993) found that seven in ten institutions reported use of TQM. For about one in ten, the use was extensive.

Administrators, staff, and even a small cadre of faculty members are intrigued by the possibilities offered by quality management. Many people on campus seem to have an intuitive kinship with some of its core principles—encouraging teamwork, improving processes and systems, using the scientific method to make decisions. Their interest is genuine.

Yet there is widespread skepticism. A recent study of twenty-one pioneering institutions (Seymour, 1993) found that people's perception that TQM was just another fad was one of the most significant hurdles to the implementation of quality management. In my own on-campus work giving speeches and seminars, I always face a vocal group of cynics at the back of the room as well as a larger number of people who are profoundly indifferent to the message.

The forces that pull and tug at our institutions are incredibly strong. We must rein in tuition increases. We must make sure that students get the classes they want when they want them. We must show that we are accountable and productive. Our constituents agree: Colleges and universities must change if they are to meet these fundamental challenges. Yet the culture of academe values tradition and the conservation of past practices. Institutional structure and values resist the whims of society while remaining true to a central mission—the creation of a knowledge base to support the evolution of our society.

We cannot continue to say to the advocates of change—board members, the parents of students, alumni, state representatives—that they do not understand us. We cannot continue to say that we are special. And we cannot dismiss the ideas that underlie TQM just because they have industrial parentage. And yet we have a responsibility to resist the latest craze, to maintain integrity and continuity within a society that is increasingly fractured by special interests and competing demands.

This sourcebook is driven by a series of puzzling contrasts. First, we need to preserve the core traditions of academe; TQM represents a fundamental shift in management philosophy and practice. Second, budget cuts mean campuses are strapped for resources; implementing TQM requires an investment of time, energy, and hard cash. Third, we cannot continue to operate our institutions according to assumptions that are no longer true; TQM may work on the factory floor, but the assumption that students are customers will not work.

The fundamental question that confronts every educator who contemplates the use of total quality management principles at his or her institution must be this: Is it worth doing? In the first chapter, I attempt to shed light on this question by reviewing data from industry and the early returns from higher education. The discussion centers on studies and research that examine the type of results that TQM has generated. I also touch on costs. A substantial portion of the chapter is devoted to the concept of return on quality investment (ROQI). This concept offers the reader practitioner a framework within which to evaluate the costs and benefits of quality management at his or her institution.

Chapters Two, Three, and Four describe methodologies that can be used for looking at performance measures within the context of cost-benefit analysis. In Chapter Two, Tom Tuttle, director of the Maryland Center for Quality and Productivity at the University of Maryland, asks, How do organizations measure the impact of total quality? He describes a methodology developed at his center that enables the management team of an organization to define its critical performance dimensions. He presents a set of metrics that, he believes, can help colleges and universities to assess whether quality management is improving their performance.

In Chapter Three, Tim Miller, the coordinator of the Quality Institute at El Camino College, describes his institution's cost-of-quality model. He details the need for such a model, describes its operational aspects, and reviews the initial pilot study. The El Camino model is a no-nonsense operationalization of the ROQI concept at a college that has years of quality management experience. As you might expect, the pilot study provokes a number of ideas and suggestions for further improvement of the model.

Chapter Four, by Barbara Lembcke of George Mason University, presents a family of organizational performance measures that enable decision makers to weigh the returns on TQM investments. She uses the enrollment management process to illustrate the use of six performance measures. She concludes that the return on such an investment cannot be evaluated properly without a thorough knowledge of organizational performance before and after the investment decision is made.

The next three chapters in this sourcebook are personal perspectives from individuals in different positions at different types of institutions: One author is president of a community college, another is a professor at a service academy, and the third is chief financial officer at a private college. Linda Thor, president of Rio Salado Community College and the author of Chapter Five, tells us that Rio Salado approached TQM from a perspective that asked, How can we produce higher-quality educational services? The resulting investment has yielded benefits that she can tick off with precision. For example, printing costs were reduced by $24,497.73. Job satisfaction measures nearly doubled in three years. She also describes other changes—more subtle, more reflective—that portray an altered culture.

In contrast to Rio Salado, the U.S. Air Force Academy never had a choice: Headquarters mandated its adoption of quality management. David Porter, a professor in the Department of Behavioral Sciences and Leadership at the academy, has helped to shape that mandate into an integrated system that delivers quality results. In Chapter Six, he describes a perspective that uses understanding and trust to facilitate organizational transformation and the consequences of quality as they relate to such levels within his institution as faculty and department.

Chapter Seven is contributed by Alan Norton, vice president for financial affairs at St. John Fisher College, an institution that has been on the leading edge of the quality movement in higher education. He notes that the CFO is the guardian who oversees the proper use of institutional resources. In that capacity, he analyzes the costs associated with the implementation of quality management at St. John Fisher and outlines a simple yet effective way of determining whether the investment is yielding an acceptable internal rate of return.

In the conclusion to this sourcebook, I encourage the reader to strike an informed balance between the hype of some well-meaning advocates of TQM and the knee-jerk negativism of the cynics at the back of the room.

Daniel Seymour
Editor

References

El-Khawas, E. *Campus Trends 1993*. Washington, D.C.: American Council on Education, 1993.

Horine, J., Hailey, W. A., and Rubach, L. "Shaping America's Future." *Quality Progress*, Oct. 1993, pp. 41–60.

Seymour, D. *Total Quality Management in Higher Education: Clearing the Hurdles*. Methuen, Mass.: GOAL/QPC, 1993.

"Special Focus: Total Quality Management on Campus." *Educational Record*, Spring 1993 (entire issue).

"TQM: Will It Work on Campus?" *Change*, May–June 1993 (entire issue).

DANIEL SEYMOUR is president of QSystems, a quality management firm in Palm Springs, California, and visiting scholar at Claremont Graduate School.

Before committing an institution to the principles of TQM, leaders should ask themselves some hard questions—for example, How much is this going to cost? How will I know if the investment is successful?

The Return on Quality Investment

Daniel Seymour

One of the most popular books on quality (Crosby, 1979, p. 1) begins: "Quality is free. It's not a gift, but it is free. What costs money are the unquality things—all the actions that involve not doing jobs right the first time." This is an important point. The costs associated with doing things wrong and then having to fix them are enormous: broken or poorly fitting parts for production processes are thrown away; improperly filled in forms are returned for correction; unanswered or incorrectly answered questions force customers to ask those questions again and again. What would happen if things were done right the first time—if there were no waste in production processes, if all form were perfectly filled in, if customers got the right answers from the first person with whom they talked?

Crosby (1979) claims that the costs associated with delivering a product or service of high quality are lower than the costs associated with low quality. Why? Because the cost of unquality—of finding and fixing mistakes—is greater than the cost of doing it right the first time.

But is quality free? No. The do-it-right-the-first-time systems and processes to which Crosby (1979) refers do not exist. They must be created from systems and processes that are currently weighed down by scrap, rework, complexity, breakdown, and delays. Such a paradigm shift requires an investment of time, energy, and money. The organization must rethink its aim; the design and management of processes must be changed; new reward systems and communication efforts must be initiated. The culture needs to be transformed. And cultural transformation does not come cheap.

This chapter, indeed this sourcebook, is concerned with the return on quality investment (ROQI) in higher education. It is simply not good enough to say that quality is free. Like their counterparts in industry, college and university officials have a fiduciary responsibility to invest their institutions' scarce resources wisely. That means that they must make an informed decision when do-it-right-the-first-time systems and processes are created. It comes down to a question like this: Is it better to invest in the management of quality—training, forming teams, collecting data, redesigning processes—or in a freshly resurfaced parking lot, new Ph.D. programs, increased travel funds for faculty, or something else?

Evidence from Industry

In industry, discussion of ROQI involves thousands of companies, millions of people, and billions of dollars. A review of TQM adoption rates found in a broad series of studies (Hiam, 1993) provides ample evidence. For instance, a survey conducted by Lakewood Research on training activities in U.S. businesses concluded that 62 percent of the firms in the sample provided employees with quality improvement training. A study by the Center for Effective Organizations at the University of Southern California investigated adoption of quality management and employee involvement practices by surveying executives of Fortune 1000 companies. Seventy-seven percent of the firms sampled had active TQM processes in place.

Hiam (1993) analyzes these two studies and eighteen others for evidence concerning the use and impact of TQM practices. One of the patterns that emerged from this qualitative meta-analysis was that large industrial firms were the first to adopt total quality management, with 75 to 80 percent of the large firms in all the studies having TQM programs. The data indicate that large service firms and midsized manufacturing firms were adopting TQM quickly and that smaller firms were the least likely to pursue TQM processes. The conclusion was that "TQM efforts—driven by the voice of the customer and achieved through techniques ranging from continuous process improvement and just-in-time manufacturing to teamwork, benchmarking, statistical process control, and employee participation—are increasing in U.S companies" (Hiam, 1993, p. 5).

All these companies, which range from Xerox and IBM to hotel chains and hospitals, have embarked on this transforming journey in the expectation that they will derive some positive benefits. None of these companies would say, "Well, it's a lot of work, but let's just do it anyway." Nor would they say, "Everyone else is doing it, so we might as well, too." The key officials in these firms have a belief or at least a strong hope that performance will be enhanced, output will increase, costs will be reduced, and customer satisfaction will improve.

But what does the evidence suggest? Can we say with any certainty that developing and implementing quality management practices is a good investment? The answer appears to be an unqualified maybe.

Some of the evidence is glowing. Ernst & Young and the American Quality Foundation surveyed 584 companies in the automotive, computer, banking, and health care industries in the United States, Canada, Germany, and

Japan. Performance was evaluated on three dimensions: profitability (measured by return on assets), productivity (measured by value added per employee), and quality (measured with an index of overall quality as perceived by end users of the respondents' products and services). The study concluded that several TQM practices—for example, process improvement methods, including cycle time analysis, process value analysis, and process simplification—are universally beneficial. That is, they have a significant impact on profitability, productivity, and quality.

Several other studies report an equally strong relationship between TQM practices and a variety of performance measures. IBM contrasted the performance of fifty-seven business units that had scored high on the Malcolm Baldrige National Quality Award criteria (for example, the use of data to inform decisions, the degree to which customer requirements are assessed) with its other business units (Hiam, 1993). The study measured performance trends in five different areas: customer satisfaction, employee morale, quality of products and services, financial results, and market share. Results indicate that units having the most deeply embedded quality practices performed better in each of the five categories.

At the request of Congressman Donald Ritter, the U.S. General Accounting Office (GAO) studied the performance of twenty-two finalists and winners of the Malcolm Baldrige award (U.S. General Accounting Office, 1991). The GAO analyzed company records to identify the annual change in a wide variety of performance measures, including employee relations, product quality, cost, customer satisfaction, market share, and profitability. The GAO concluded that "companies that adopted quality management practices experienced an overall improvement in corporate performance" (U.S. General Accounting Office, 1991, p. 2). Employees experienced increased job satisfaction, attendance improved, and employee turnover decreased. Companies increased the reliability and on-time delivery of their product or service and reduced errors, product lead time, and the cost of quality. Consumers' overall perceptions about a product or service and customer retention rates improved, while the number of complaints received decreased. Finally, profitability, as measured by several ratios widely used in financial analysis, improved.

Other studies have reported more mixed results. For example, a survey by the consulting firm Rath & Strong (Hiam, 1993) asked executives of Fortune 500 companies to identify objectives for TQM within their organizations and to state whether TQM had had a major impact on their efforts to meet those objectives. The results, shown in Table 1.1, suggest that TQM had a significant impact on many corporate objectives, including increased competitiveness and market share. But the results also suggest that TQM accomplishments fall short of management goals for TQM in many companies. Indeed, while almost one-fifth of the respondents said that their company had met all its objectives and 45 percent that the company had achieved more than one-half of its objectives, almost two-fifths—38 percent—reported their firm had to date achieved none of the objectives of its TQM efforts.

Table 1.1. TQM Objectives and Impact

Executives' Ranking of Objectives According to Importance	*Percentage Who Think Objective Was Accomplished*
1. Respond to increased competition	44%
2. Increase market share	39
3. Satisfy more demanding customers	62
4. Reduce costs	49
5. Decrease time to market	41
6. Create a more satisfying workplace	54
7. Stem loss of market share	30
8. Recruit/retain employees	27

Source: Adapted from Hiam, 1993, p. 26.

A number of studies and reports have reached generally negative conclusions. For example, Booz Allen & Hamilton concluded from a qualitative review of client companies (Hiam, 1993) that TQM efforts had been abandoned or redefined in many instances. The Health Care Advisory Board (*TQM: The Second Generation,* 1992) reviews the results of two studies: a survey by Arthur D. Little survey of 500 institutions in which only one in three respondents felt that TQM had had significant impact on the firm's competitiveness and a survey of 100 British firms by A.T. Kearney in which 80 percent of the respondents believed that TQM had failed to achieve tangible results. These studies, combined with its own anecdotal insights, led the advisory board to conclude that there was no compelling evidence that TQM was a break-even proposition. Moreover, the vast majority of institutions in these two surveys reported small or no results. The review concluded that even the most committed practitioners cannot prove that business upticks are tied to TQM.

In general, then, the research shows a significant and growing number of companies are using quality management principles. Some report strong results, others have found mixed results, and still others are clearly struggling to generate a meaningful impact on performance. To muddy the issue a bit more, in most of the studies the term *results* is not to be interpreted as net results—that is, as benefits minus the costs incurred to generate the benefits. For example, the IBM study concluded that business units scoring high on the Baldrige criteria also performed better in some unspecified way on each of five performance measures. But what does that really mean?

As stated earlier, the shift to a quality-driven operating environment requires a significant investment of time, energy, and money. There are training and materials expenses. Then teams are formed. The teams meet regularly, collect data, analyze work flows, generate action plans, and test implementation strategies. All this is typically done in addition to the regular work. Further, there is usually a centralized office staffed by a director, trainers, and facilitators to coordinate these efforts. The point is, of course, that increased customer satisfaction or improved employee morale does not come without a cost—or an investment. IBM invested in quality management to achieve results. Was it worth it? Would $20,000 in costs yielding a 10 percent increase in customer satisfaction be a good investment? Probably. How about a $2 million investment that led to a 5 percent change? Maybe not.

U.S. General Accounting Office (1991) is another example. Improved employee relations, customer satisfaction, and product quality are noteworthy and laudable achievements. But we do not know what it cost to achieve these results. Even the stated increase in market share and decrease in costs are problematic. As any businessperson can tell you, it is relatively easy to boost market share even as you slip slowly into bankruptcy. Looking at costs alone can also be deceiving. Costs can be cut to the point that has a devastating effect on revenues—product or service quality is sacrificed. The one business measure that does capture a net result is profitability. The problem with profitability or other bottom-line measures is that it is difficult if not impossible to establish causality. Can we be certain that our investment in quality was the key factor in increased profitability, not the fact that a major competitor went out of business?

The only study or report to look explicitly at the cost side of the ledger is that of the Health Care Advisory Board (*TQM: The Second Generation,* 1992). After reviewing the expenses associated with quality initiatives, the report describes a typical start-up budget, which is illustrated in Table 1.2. These and other data lead the author to state that, "despite its growing popularity, TQM may be a multimillion-dollar mistake; many hospital executives betting the bank (and their careers) on TQM are spending hundreds of thousands for start-up, millions for ongoing expenses" (*TQM: The Second Generation,* 1992, p. 2).

Quality Management on Campus

Reality hit the automobile industry in the 1980s: The Japanese were producing better cars at more affordable prices. The same reality hit the electronics, textile, and aeronautic industries. Health care was next. Each industry suffered from bloated bureaucracies, stifling policies, inflated costs, and questionable quality. Many of our industries were ill, and TQM was viewed as the cure.

Higher education in this country is not well, either. We have many of the same health problems that our industrial colleagues are facing. So it is not surprising that educators—many at the urging of board members from industry—have looked at TQM as a possible remedy.

Two studies have explored the degree to which the TQM remedy has been applied to campuses. The American Council on Education conducts an annual survey of changes taking place in the academic and administrative practices of American colleges and universities. According to the most recent survey (El-Khawas, 1993, p. 17), "survey results show that many campuses are considering how TQM, or other quality improvement techniques, might apply to their programs." The report goes on to state that seven in ten institutions

Table 1.2. Typical TQM Start-Up Costs

	Year 1	*Year 2*	*Year 3*
Salary and Benefits	$72,000	$91,520	$95,181
Quality coordinator (1 FTE)	40,000	41,600	43,264
Trainers (.5 FTE)	16,000	16,640	17,306
Team facilitators (1 FTE)	16,000	33,280	34,611
Training and Education	$26,000	$10,000	$11,000
Participant training materials audiovisual, support equipment	1,000	2,000	3,000
External seminars, conferences	25,000	8,000	8,000
Travel	$17,000	$16,500	$16,500
External seminars, conferences	6,000	10,500	10,500
Site visits	5,000	0	0
Network meetings	6,000	6,000	6,000
Rewards and Recognition	$1,000	$2,000	$4,000
In-House Communication	$1,000	$2,000	$4,000
Consulting Services	$15,000	$9,000	$5,000
Indirect Expenses	$27,402	$48,376	$65,912
Training hours	9,584	26,992	43,704
Team participation	2,106	8,424	16,848
Internal resource hours	15,712	12,960	5,360
Total	$159,402	$179,396	$201,593

Note: This budget assumes 75 upper-level managers trained in years 1 and 2 with an 8-hour course; 1,200 employees oriented in years 2 and 3 with a 2-hour course; and facilitators trained with a 40-hour course. It also assumes 3 pilot teams in year 1; 12 teams in year 2; and 24 teams in year 3.

Source: TQM: The Second Generation, 1992, p. 42.

reported use of TQM. However, for six in ten, these activities were limited in scope. About one in one institutions reported extensive use of TQM. Two-year colleges were the most likely to report that their TQM activities were extensive.

Quality Progress, a publication of the American Society for Quality Control, has conducted a survey of quality management efforts in educational institutions for the past several years. The most recent survey (Horine, Hailey, and Rubach, 1993) describes the activities of 139 universities and 46 community colleges. The findings suggest the degree to which quality management efforts have penetrated these institutions. Most institutions (78 percent of the universities and 70 percent of the community colleges) reported that they were in the early stages of TQM. Both two- and four-year institutions reported that fewer than 25 percent of their employees were involved in TQM efforts.

Approximately half of the institutions (50 percent of the universities and 41 percent of the community colleges) had quality councils, officers, or centers to coordinate their TQM efforts.

These measures of the breadth and depth of TQM activities on college campuses do not begin to approach the numbers from industry. However, there is every reason to believe that more and more initiatives will occur in the future as institutions continue to look for ways to improve service and control costs.

But what about results? What do our colleges and universities have to show for their early quality-related efforts? While the evidence is thin, there have been several initial efforts to look across institutions and assess ROQI in higher education. Seymour and Collett (1991) detail the work done at twenty-two pioneering institutions. These authors examine the circumstances that prompted institutions to explore TQM, the areas within institutions using TQM, the implementation plans that institutions are following, the process improvement efforts that they have initiated, and the tools that they have found to be of most use. The investigators also sought information specifically about results. For example, one section of the survey asked respondents, What are the key benefits of TQM so far? Figure 1.1 summarizes the reported benefits.

In a follow-up study, Seymour (1993) describes the ten major hurdles that twenty-one institutions are facing in their efforts to implement quality management (QM). The report also enumerates strategies to overcome these hurdles. A results-driven strategy is described by Seymour as the institutional response to three different hurdles. For instance, one dominant hurdle involves

Figure 1.1. What Are the Key Benefits of TQM So Far?

Give people a voice: "People feel a new emphasis on their value and input."

Less explaining, more listening: "The focus on customers rather than self has caused staff to stop spending so much time explaining and start listening to what customers want."

Cutting down on steps: "We have cut down on bureaucratic steps, the number of signatures on travel forms and work orders, and so on."

A change in climate: "There is a new sense of hope among our staff that all our processes can be improved and that life in the office will get better."

A willingness to sweat the details: "We've observed a definite decrease in solution jumping."

Bringing people together: "There is a wonderful new sense of camaraderie that I can only attribute to the fact that we know each other better now."

A common language: "The staff now have a common language to share their frustrations and their concerns with each other without involving personalities."

Knowing what we are about: "We are more goal directed. We have a better sense of purpose that seems to translate into more committed action."

Reduced scrap and rework: "We now know what waste is all about and how we can analyze our work to reduce it."

Declining dollars: "I know that our mailing costs were reduced by one-third. Later, when a person left, we did not replace her."

Source: Seymour and Collett, 1991.

individuals' being so overloaded that they cannot contemplate taking on the additional time commitment and responsibilities of TQM. One of the strategies described by survey respondents suggests that "the best way to overcome the 'time' hurdle . . . is to choose improvement projects that have shorter completion times and offer tangible results. . . . People need to see the connection between the time they are investing and actions that will be taken" (Seymour, 1993, p. 5).

Another hurdle involves the difficulty of overcoming many people's perception that this is just another fad that will dry up and blow away. The results-driven strategy used to respond to this hurdle is described as follows: "The dominant strategic response to this problem is to generate results that are impossible to ignore. This strategy is best summed up by the president of one institution who remarked, 'You cannot argue with results'" (Seymour, 1993, p. 9). He and others suggested that bottom-line results—saving money, reducing cycle time, increasing customer satisfaction—were the most effective way to clear the 'fad' hurdle.

Political problems are the third hurdle. There are a few people on campus who not only do not agree with QM but who work to talk it down. Again, one of the major strategies articulated by respondents focuses on results: "This strategy simply suggests that it may be more appropriate to concentrate on changing behaviors first, attitudes second. The best way to do this is to push hard on generating results—monetary savings, reducing cycle time, creating easier-to-use forms and processes and so on." It then states that the results-driven strategy is effective in dealing with political problems because, "when you go for results, they are much harder to talk down than concepts" (Seymour, 1993, p. 19).

Finally, Horine, Hailey, Rubach (1993) discuss process improvement efforts briefly. Most of their attention is directed to areas (for example, administration, maintenance, purchasing) in which improvement efforts have taken place, but they also share anecdotes illustrating the type of results that can be achieved; for example, "Harvard University's Office of Information Technology has more than forty teams pursuing quality improvement in the administrative areas. These teams achieved an 85 percent reduction in data entry error rate in Harvard's copy services, a 20 percent productivity gain in data center operations, and an annual $60,000 savings in expenses on network services area traffic" (Horine, Hailey, Rubach, 1993, p. 43).

Certainly all these statements and examples of results are encouraging. But, as I noted in the section focused on industry, results do not necessarily mean net results. Nothing in these discussions of results or strategies tells us what institutions are investing. An 85 percent reduction in the data entry error rate is impressive, as is a 20 percent productivity gain. Reducing costs by $60,000 is exactly the type of result that colleges and universities need in an era of inflationary tuition rates. Unfortunately, none of these metrics says anything about return as a function of investment.

One of the few attempts to generate insight into ROQI in higher education comes from the study by Seymour and Collett (1991). One of the last questions asked in their survey was this: "From a cost-benefit perspective, has it been worth it so far?" The responses fell equally into two categories: on the one hand, it's too early to tell; on the other, unconditionally yes. For those in the too-early-to-tell group, start-up costs were outdistancing results: "Because we are still so early in the process of adopting quality management techniques and strategies, we are expending more effort than we are receiving in benefits" (Seymour and Collett, 1991, p. 25). "TQM has been extremely costly, particularly when training members . . . [and] the number of identifiable TQM projects ha[s] been minimal; therefore currently the cost has not been offset by the benefits" (Seymour and Collett, 1991, p. 25).

The unconditional-yes group was dominated by two types of responses: one emotional, the other more studied and analytical. Here are two of the responses that speak from the heart: "Definitely. This is causing people to think, to challenge their paradigms in all areas, and to celebrate change rather than fear it. It has also helped flatten the decision-making hierarchy" (Seymour and Collett, 1991, p. 25). "It has certainly been worth the cost and effort so far . . . moving our department from a 1960s style operation into one with at least a mid-1980s mode. And we're accomplishing major improvement in our culture" (Seymour and Collett, 1991, p. 25).

In contrast, other respondents looked at their experiences from a cost-benefit perspective and attempted to think in terms of dollars and performance measures. These comments reflect this more analytical approach: "To date, I would estimate that, in its two years of implementation, we have invested approximately $100,000 in the implementation process. These are real dollars that have been diverted from the regular campus budget to implement total quality management . . . I am 100 percent committed to its [continued] implementation . . . it has been worth the money and effort because TQM has greatly improved the culture of the campus" (Seymour and Collett, 1991, p. 25). "Team meetings have accounted for nearly 18 percent of the time (and personnel budget) in the safety office over the last year—$6,169 in personnel time (eight persons, seven FTEs) have been devoted directly to team training. Excluding training, a minimum of $28,731 of employee time has been spent in team processes. . . . Feedback about the office and internal perceptions within the office have been positive" (Seymour and Collett, 1991, p. 25).

None of the respondents suggested that the investment had not been worth it. There are explanations for this unanimity, which is encouraging though slightly too good to be true. One explanation is that the too-early-to-tell responses temporarily conceal a slew of no answers. This explanation is reasonable given that many of the institutions were described as neophytes with less than three years of experience. Another explanation is wishful thinking on the part of a small group of trailblazers: "They [the respondents] have spent tremendous time and energy learning about total quality management principles and tools and are unable or unwilling to believe that it has not been worth it" (Seymour and Collett, 1991, p. 25). Finally, it is plausible to conclude that many respondents believe on some gut level that the costs will be worth it. They may not be able to prove it yet, but they believe it just the same.

In connection with this *New Directions in Higher Education* volume, I sent a survey instrument called the Quality Quotient to individuals at sixty institutions actively engaged in applying quality management principles to their operations. Each of these individuals had been identified as the person having the most knowledge of campus initiatives. Fifty-two responses were received, for an 87 percent response rate.

Participants were asked to rate six statements on a five-point scale ranging from strongly disagree (SD) to strongly agree (SA). The data were analyzed as both composite scores and by the number of years for which the respondent's division or institution had been actively pursuing a quality approach. The fifteen novice institutions had one or two years of such experience, the twenty-eight intermediate institutions had three to four years, and the nine most experienced institutions had five or more years.

STATEMENT 1: *We have made a public commitment to operating under quality principles.*

This statement and the next refer to investment. In this case, the investment is a political one—making a public commitment to the use of quality principles to operate the institution. The novice institutions are under the average (3.7), the intermediate institutions are at the average (4.1), and the most experienced institutions are considerably above average (4.6). These responses reflect the changing confidence levels of institutional leaders: The longer they have been at it, the more willing they are to make public proclamations.

STATEMENT 2: *We have made a significant investment of time, energy, and money in our quality efforts.*

The average was 4.0, equivalent to *I agree.* This statement yielded the highest rating in the survey—4.8—which came from the institutions that had the greatest experience. Obviously, these institutions are keenly aware that their investment in quality management over the years has been significant. The responses of novices averaged out to 3.5 and of intermediates to 3.9.

STATEMENT 3: *To date, I am personally very satisfied with our quality initiatives.*

This statement and the next reflect a broad view of results. Overall, the respondents show mild agreement (3.7). The novice institutions and the intermediate institutions have identical scores of 3.5. The experienced institutions are at 4.5—a significant jump. The difference can be explained in a number of ways. The most appealing explanation is that it takes time before people begin to see results that they are willing to describe as satisfying.

STATEMENT 4: *Our quality improvement results have been very strong.*

The average for this statement was 3.2. It generated a 2.7 response from the novice institutions. The response edges across neutral for the intermediate institutions (3.1). The most experienced institutions in the survey were right on the agree mark (4.0).

STATEMENT 5: *We have developed and we use a methodology to measure costs and benefits associated with our quality initiative.*

This statement and the next attempt sought information about the degree to which institutions have a specific methodology for analyzing ROQI. While the range of responses to the preceding statements was fairly wide between novice and experienced institutions, the responses to this statement collapse around the mean of 2.9. The least experienced institutions are at 2.7, the intermediates at 2.9, and the most experienced at 3.0.

STATEMENT 6: *We can demonstrate a positive net return (the benefits outweigh the costs) on our investment in quality.*

The last statement reflects the stark reality of an ROQI perspective. It asks, in effect, Can you show, with numbers, that it is worth doing? Again, the data for the three levels of experience collapse about a mean (2.1) centered just slightly above *I disagree.* The range is from 2.0 to 2.2.

Barriers to an ROQI Mind-set

As the pressures on higher education continue to mount and as books, articles, speeches, and conference sessions tell TQM success stories, increasing numbers of institutions will be tempted to adopt total quality management practices. It may be board members who provide the incentive. Or a dean and a few faculty members may decide to explore the works of Deming, Juran, Crosby, and Ishikawa. A director may read about one of the winners of the Baldrige award and conclude that the possibility of reducing costs while increasing customer satisfaction is worth a careful look. All the events just cited as possibilities have in fact taken place, and they will continue to take place in the near future.

But while the potential is real and the possibilities are significant, there are also some fundamental problems. Perhaps the most serious problem is manifest in the results of the survey that I conducted for this chapter. The first two statements reflect the investment—of time, energy, money, and commitment—that colleges and universities have made in a quality management approach. The data suggest that the respondents believe that the investment is significant. Moreover, the data show that the investment increases over time.

The third statement is a general measure of satisfaction with the institution's quality initiative. The respondents agree with the statement. The fourth statement focuses on results, and it is obvious that enthusiasm is waning. Costs, benefits, and measures are textual in the fifth statement. The results here reflect increasing uncertainty about the effects of the investment in quality. The last statement asks if the institution can prove that the investment is paying off. The answer is no. The conclusion that we must draw is that it is a great deal easier to make a commitment to quality than it is to demonstrate that the investment decision was a wise one.

A similar conclusion can be derived from the Health Care Advisory Board report (*TQM: The Second Generation,* 1992). This review of numerous studies in the health care industry resulted in a number of stark observations. Several are relevant to the present discussion: The biggest surprise was that, despite the absence of results, many health care executives were pleased with TQM progress and certain that big results were just a few months or years away. The authors of the report felt that the results hoped for were unlikely to materialize. At many hospitals, TQM was more about appearance than substance. Moreover, hospitals were being lulled into a false sense of security by the bustle of activity associated with TQM (staff are trained, teams are organized). They failed to realize that team efforts were not contributing to the bottom line. The authors of the report believed that the failure of these efforts to produce results was not an inherent weakness of TQM but was due to a combination of basic misunderstanding about what TQM can achieve with faulty implementation. Finally, the most important reason why TQM seems destined to disappoint is that a great many hospitals fundamentally misunderstand TQM because they confuse TQM—the means to an end—improvement—with the end itself.

These observations, combined with the results from the Quality Quotient study, produce a number of insights into ROQI. The first insight is that the leadership in both health care and higher education shows a disturbing tendency to think that, just because their people are talking about it, they are doing it. There is a tendency to make public commitments that, on reflection, are more about the appearance of reform and change than anything else. Speeches are made, vision statements are rewritten, and lapel buttons are distributed. The declaration is dutiful and forceful—this organization is now for quality. Unfortunately, speeches do not change a culture. It requires individuals—lots of them—to begin to think and act differently.

Next, the organization unleashes TQM. There is an investment in developing an office of quality that has a director, a secretary, telephones, and a letterhead. Then the training begins. Teams are formed, meetings are held, and reports are written. A quality newsletter may be produced. All this activity can make it easy to lose sight of the aim: to improve performance. Means become ends, and the notion of a return on the investment in quality gets lost in all the memos and meetings. The result is that the number of people trained emerges as a measure of success for the organization, while other, more important metrics involving customer satisfaction, cycle time, and costs fade into the background.

Why do organizations have such difficulty pursuing the ROQI mind-set? How do organizations get into the position of having invested large sums of time, energy, and money in a quality initiative that gives them little if anything substantive to show for their efforts? From the studies and the reports cited earlier, the answer involves three parts: leadership, implementation, and measurement.

Leadership. The first part of the answer takes dead aim at leadership. The leaders of our organizations shape the vision and tell us what it will take to get there. To help us get from where we are now to where we need to go, leaders must know a great deal about the risks, costs, and benefits associated with the new direction. They must possess a bone-deep understanding of the journey's pathway.

Total quality management is much more than a list of points, a dozen or so statistical tools, and slogans that exhort employees to improve their work performance. It is a paradigm shift. The current managers of higher education are attempting to introduce a fundamentally different way of thinking and acting into an existing culture that has well-defined rules, standards, and protocols. When fresh and new ideas run smack into an existing culture, the status quo almost always wins. That is why leadership is critical to change. As Joel Barker (1992, p. 164) states, "You manage within a paradigm. You lead between paradigms."

The leadership required for the shift to a quality-driven paradigm is leadership that knows precisely what is at stake and that can articulate the issues. Let us deal first with the investment side of the equation. Part of the investment is in the materials and time devoted to process improvement projects. The other part of the investment is in knowledge creation. Faculty, staff, and administrators who work on improvement teams must be trained in the tools and techniques of quality management. But perhaps even more important, the leadership must be willing to make a sincere and time-consuming effort to help people understand the philosophy.

Then there is the return side of the equation. Only the leadership can set mind-stretching goals for a quality initiative and focus the institution's attention on improvement and innovation. The leadership must be able to express dissatisfaction with the status quo and foster the development of a critical mass of followers who are just as uncomfortable with the ways things are today. Further, leaders must energize the institution to pursue new aims for tomorrow.

Thus, the development of an ROQI mind-set within an institution depends on the ability of its leaders to understand the real costs and benefits associated with TQM. They must also be willing to use that understanding in day-to-day decision making.

Implementation. The second part of the explanation is easy to derive from a cursory review of the TQM studies reported earlier. It follows closely on the heels of the leadership issue. In order to develop an ROQI mind-set, there must be a full understanding of the dynamics of implementation. Time and again, it has been shown that the failure of TQM to improve performance is a function of poor implementation. The prophecy is self-fulfilling. If leaders do not invest their own time in knowledge development, in planning and articulating the change strategy, the philosophy is poorly operationalized. Is it any wonder that organizations find they have nothing to show for their efforts after years of struggle?

We know the barriers. Seymour (1993) provides ample evidence: People perceive that TQM is just another fad. Supervisors and administrators are reluctant to let go of decision-making power. Leaders repeatedly get distracted from quality issues. We also know what works. There is ample evidence to guide us in the paradigm shift.

What is needed is a methodology to make it happen. There must be a strategic perspective, fueled by political courage, to move from the theory of TQM to the practice of never-ending improvement of work processes. Such a strategic orientation makes the notion of ROQI come alive. It says, in effect: These are the kinds of things I need to do in order to ensure that my investment will pay off in the long run. Without such an orientation, there is no connection between the costs associated with the pursuit of quality and the benefits that we need to derive from any reallocation of scarce organizational resources.

Measurement. The final piece of the puzzle is measurement. An ROQI mind-set involves the active management of costs and benefits. But you cannot manage what you do not measure. On the investment side of the equation, higher education has done little to understand or control costs. The philosophy has been to generate as much revenue as possible, then spend it. The operating budgets at most institutions are driven by full-time-equivalent student reimbursement, which focuses the attention of institutions on growth and revenue enhancement. Thus, activity-based cost accounting—an approach that assigns costs to processes instead of functional areas—is well developed in industry, but it has yet to make a dent in the business offices of colleges and universities.

Then there is the return on investment. A question that I often ask in my seminars and workshops is this: How do you know if you are successful? It seems reasonable to expect leaders to be able to describe the vital signs of their organizations. They should be able to quantify how well the activities that go into a process or the outputs of a process achieve a specified aim. Yet the question usually generates blank stares instead of operational indicators, shuffling feet instead of metrics.

Should not institutions be able to measure the return on their investment in quality? This issue is not as clear-cut as the leadership and implementation issues. Recall Figure 1.1. Many of the benefits described by the pioneering colleges and universities—giving people a voice, the willingness to sweat details, the development of a common language—do not submit easily to quantification. W. Edwards Deming (1982) makes this point throughout his classic book, *Out of the Crisis*. He credits Lloyd Nelson, the director of statistical methods for the Nashua Corporation, with having said that the most important figures needed for management of any organization are unknown and unknowable. In effect, it is a mistake to manage by visible figures alone. So much of what is truly important—for example, giving people a voice—cannot be measured in conventional ways. However, it must also be noted that Deming (1982, p. 121) goes on to say that successful managers "must nevertheless take account of them [the unknown and unknowable figures]."

Perhaps the best way to pursue the measurement issue is to ask the question, How will you know if your investment in quality is successful? Then begin to struggle with the answers. Measure costs and performance wherever possible. Do not try to quantify the things that are unknowable, but do not forget that there are knowable and quantifiable vital signs that you can generate. In fact, the very act of measuring something can often produce insight into the blindingly obvious and yield almost instant improvements.

You Must Swim, Too

One of Aesop's fables is called "The Shipwreck." It goes like this: A rich man was on a voyage across the sea when a terrible storm blew up. The rich man's ship capsized, and everyone was thrown into the sea. All the passengers then began to swim for their lives, except the rich man, who raised his arms to heaven and called to the goddess Athena, offering her all kinds of riches if she would save him. The other passengers soon reached pieces of wreckage and, clinging to them, shouted back to the praying man: "Don't leave it all to the goddess. You must swim, too."

While higher education may not be shipwrecked, there is no doubt that it is being battered by a storm of failing public trust. Our colleges and universities, long immune from criticism, are being asked to justify their skyrocketing tuition rates, their inability to graduate students on time, and their seeming indifference to undergraduate education. An increasing number of institutions have decided to invoke the TQM gods to save them, that is, to make them appear to be credible, well-managed, high-performing organizations. But, as the studies reviewed in this chapter all too plainly show, making a public commitment to quality is insufficient to the task at hand. Despite brilliant rhetoric and willing spirits, many organizations have struggled to create fundamental change through total quality management.

We need to approach TQM from a return-on-quality-investment orientation. Such an orientation has its own prerequisites: Leadership must invest in its own knowledge creation. A change strategy must be implemented. Performance measures must be identified whenever possible. In effect, it is not enough to declare that you are for quality—you must swim, too.

References

Barker, J. A. *Future Edge.* New York: Morrow, 1992.

Crosby, P. *Quality Is Free.* New York: New American Library, 1979.

Deming, W. E. *Out of the Crisis.* Cambridge, Mass.: Center for Advanced Engineering Study, Massachusetts Institute of Technology, 1982.

El-Khawas, E. *Campus Trends 1993.* Washington, D.C.: American Council on Education, 1993.

Hiam, A. *Does Quality Work? A Review of Relevant Studies.* New York: The Conference Board, 1993.

Horine, J., Hailey, W. A., and Rubach, L. "Shaping America's Future." *Quality Progress,* Oct. 1993, pp. 41–60.

Seymour, D. *Total Quality Management in Higher Education: Clearing the Hurdles.* Methuen, Mass.: GOAL/QPC, 1993.

Seymour, D., and Collett, C. *Total Quality Management in Higher Education: A Critical Assessment.* Methuen, Mass.: GOAL/QPC, 1991.

TQM: The Second Generation. Washington, D.C.: Health Care Advisory Board, 1992.

U.S. General Accounting Office. *U.S. Companies Improve Performance Through Quality Efforts.* Washington, D.C.: U.S. General Accounting Office, 1991.

DANIEL SEYMOUR is president of QSystems, a quality management firm in Palm Springs, California, and visiting scholar at Claremont Graduate School.

Demonstrating the payoff of total quality in institutions of higher education may require the development of improved output and outcome indicators.

Is Total Quality Worth the Effort? How Do We Know?

Thomas C. Tuttle

Total quality continues to grow and evolve as a management strategy in industry and government (Jacob, 1993; Hiam, 1993). As a sea change in management thinking, this phenomenon might be characterized as having had four discernable stages. First there was awareness and a few early experimenters. This was followed by a blind following stage characterized by frenzied activity. Virtually all large organizations made some efforts to launch a total quality effort. Since many of these implementations were ill conceived, there were failures and disappointments. This produced a third stage of negative skepticism, which may now be ending. This is likely to be followed by a maturity stage in which the momentum continues and adoption activities are well informed. Organizations will maintain control of the process, and the strategic linkages will be made much more clearly before new or expanded efforts are launched.

An important issue in these later two stages is this: How do we determine whether total quality is producing positive results? How do we decide if the difficult personal and organizational changes required for a total quality initiative are worth the effort? This chapter adopts a boundary-spanning approach to discuss this question. First, we will examine experiences from industry and government. Then I will draw the implications for higher education.

Why Do Organizations Introduce Total Quality?

Before we can consider how leaders determine whether total quality pays off for their organization, we must understand why the approach was introduced in the first place. Only then can we determine what the expectations are and what the measurements should be.

The reasons for adopting a total quality approach have in common the desire to improve the performance of the organization. Beyond that overarching goal, the specific motivations relate to the unique circumstances specific to each organization. By subdividing organizations into manufacturing, service, and government, we can see some commonalities within sectors. However, to understand the true motivation, we must ultimately look more specifically to the level of the individual firm.

Manufacturing. In general, manufacturing organizations are experiencing strong international and domestic competition, demands from customers for reduced time between orders and shipments, shortened product life cycles, environmental pressures, and rising costs that place pressure on labor-management relations (for example, when workers are asked to shoulder an increased portion of health care costs or adopt more flexible work rules). Customer expectations for quality are also increasing.

Total quality is viewed as a strategy that can help organizations simultaneously to increase quality and decrease costs and transaction times. This performance improvement should show up in indicators of customer satisfaction, financial results, and operational results. The implementation of total quality must also recognize that employees are the source of the improvements in operational results and therefore ensure that gains in customer satisfaction are not achieved at the expense of employees. If implemented appropriately, total quality also leads to improved satisfaction for employees.

Service. To generalize to the wide range of organizations that the service industry comprises, which extend from retail and transportation to health and financial services, is very difficult. However, it is fair to say that competitive pressures are no less severe in the service industries than they are in manufacturing. In most service industries, customer retention is closely linked with profitability, and it is therefore a focus of total quality strategies. Service industries also feel pressure from restructuring, shifting and uncertain regulatory requirements (at least in banking and health care), and the need to blend information technology as an enabling tool that allows people to deliver outstanding service. Service industries also experience strong cost pressures along with the need to streamline processes to improve efficiency, cost, and customer service. Perhaps more than manufacturers, service industries must focus on skill development of frontline people who have direct customer contact (for example, telephone service representatives, bank tellers, flight attendants, sales staff). Manufacturing organizations strive to reduce variability in the manufacturing process so as to achieve a consistent outcome. In contrast, service industries must often increase variability in service-giving behaviors in order to achieve a consistent outcome. This is due to the variable requirements of the service customer. Since the interactions between frontline workers and their customers tend to mirror the workers' views of how they are treated by their employer, employee satisfaction has more immediate strategic implications for the service firm than it does for the manufacturing firm.

Given this scenario, one would look for benefits of total quality in the service industry in customer retention, customer satisfaction, operational improvements (such as cost reduction, increased productivity, reduced rework), financial improvements, and employee satisfaction.

Government. The public sector has much in common with the service industry. However, except for services that could be contracted out to the private sector, competition is not as direct a notion for government agencies as it is for private business. Nevertheless, President Clinton's plan to reinvent government (Gore, 1993) will place much more pressure and focus on competitive performance.

Perhaps the most compelling force facing managers in the public sector is the growing gap between the expectations of public agencies and their funding. In the past, the general view was that resources would be added as responsibilities and accountability were added. Today, that connection has largely been broken. Most agencies forecast a dramatically increasing demand for what they do over the next five years. However, they forecast a flat or declining rate of increase in the resources that they receive to meet those growing demands. This growing mismatch is a driving force in efforts to consider new ways of working, and total quality provides a strategy for coping with this pressure.

The preceding considerations suggest that the indicators for total quality in the public sector are efficiency, cost improvement, customer satisfaction, and employee satisfaction. In essence, these are the same indicators that are relevant for service and manufacturing industries.

How Do Organizations Measure the Impact of Total Quality?

One of the first studies investigating the impact of total quality on corporate performance was conducted by the U.S. General Accounting Office (GAO) (U.S. General Accounting Office, 1991). This report examined the impact of total quality in terms of the following four categories of performance measures:

Employee-Related Indicators
Employee satisfaction
Attendance
Turnover
Safety/health
Suggestions received

Operating Indicators
Reliability
Timeliness of delivery
Order-processing time
Errors or defects
Product lead time
Inventory turnover
Costs of quality
Cost savings

Customer Satisfaction
Overall customer satisfaction
Customer complaints
Customer retention

Financial Performance Indicators
Market share
Sales per employee
Return on assets
Return on sales

The report concluded that "performance indicators in each area GAO studied showed an overall average annual improvement from the time the companies adopted total quality management to the publication of the latest available data" (U.S. General Accounting Office, 1991, p. 3).

Inherent in the philosophy of total quality is that its scope is total in the sense of organizational performance. As the GAO performance variables just enumerated imply, total quality impacts all aspects of performance. As a strategic management philosophy, total quality should have a positive impact on the strategic performance dimensions that are critical for organizational success. Each organization must define its own specific set of performance dimensions as part of its strategic planning process.

The Maryland Center for Quality and Productivity at the University of Maryland has developed a methodology called *strategic performance measurement methodology* (SPMM) that leads the management team of an organization to define these critical performance dimensions (Sink and Tuttle, 1989; Tuttle and Romanowski, 1985; Tuttle and Weaver, 1986; Tuttle, 1991). In the SPMM, these dimensions are referred to as *key result areas*. An engineering consulting firm identified seven key result areas: internal and external customer satisfaction; teamwork and entrepreneurship; technical excellence and innovation; an image of corporate excellence; pride, job satisfaction, and employee commitment; continuous improvement of quality; and financial success ensuring long-term stability and growth. A gas utility company defined four key result areas: customer satisfaction, financial success, employee satisfaction, and market leadership. A property and casualty insurance company enumerated five: customer retention and satisfaction, control of underwriting profits and losses, employee satisfaction and retention, return on equity and a disciplined balance sheet, and low costs and high operating efficiency.

While the key result areas are not performance indicators, they identify the categories within which performance indicators are developed. The purpose of key result areas in the measurement process is to ensure that performance measures are aligned with the business strategy. Since resources tend to flow from unmeasured areas of performance to areas that are measured, it is vital for organizations to measure the right things. *Right* is defined as those aspects of performance that are essential for competitive success or for accomplishing the organization's mission.

Kaplan and Norton (1992, 1993) have a similar perspective on organizational measurement. They use a device called the *balanced scorecard* to provide a semistructured organization-wide approach that ensures a balance between the concerns of various stakeholders. The approach defines four categories of performance called *perspectives*—financial, customer, internal business, and innovation and learning—within which the organization develops goals and performance measures. The balanced scorecard forces organizations to integrate nonfinancial with financial measures. And the innovation and learning perspective promotes a future orientation through its concern with the organization's ability to improve continually and create value.

Hronec (1993) has proposed another perspective on measurement. This approach, called *quantum performance*, is a performance management model that attempts to align measurement activities under three headings: cost, time, and quality. One strength of the quantum performance model is that it promotes alignment from top to bottom, and it recognizes that measures must be developed specifically at each organizational level. That is, the cost measures for an organizational division are not simply the result of rolling up the cost measures from the individual sections or departments within the division but are qualitatively different. A division is more than the sum of its parts. As an approach to evaluation of the impact of total quality, the model has some weaknesses. It does not focus sufficiently on customer metrics, and it proposes a very limited view of quality as "goodness." Most authorities on total quality have rejected this view. They argue that quality must be defined by the customer and that measures of quality must determine whether customer expectations or requirements have been met or exceeded. Hronec (1993) does stress that the output measures selected must align with customer expectations, but he does not describe a methodology that can ensure such alignment.

These approaches to performance measurement have several common features that help to define the criteria for judging a performance measurement system. First, there should be a direct relationship between the mission and strategy of the organization and what the performance measurement system measures. This is the issue of strategic alignment. Second, the measurement system must contain a number of separate indicators that address the critical facets of the mission and strategy. Third, this family of measures should address a variety of perspectives including internal organizational issues and external perspectives (for example, customer behavior and reactions); both financial and nonfinancial measures; and both past and future perspectives, such as Kaplan and Norton's (1992, 1993) learning and innovation dimensions. Fourth, for the measurement scheme to produce organizational alignment, it should be easy to explain and understand. Therefore, complex weighted indices and a large number of measures should be rejected. The measurement system will have the desired communication and focusing effect only if a broad segment of organizational members understand it. And the measurement system must, of course, take into account the normal technical considerations for measurement, such as reliability and validity.

So how do organizations know if total quality is working? Total quality is working if the organization is improving its competitive position and if it can sustain that improvement over time. Thus, we can only assess the effectiveness of total quality in terms of overall organizational success. For Xerox, one example of total quality success was its ability to win back market share that it had lost to Japanese firms. For Ford Motor Company, measures of success included its ability to increase market share and to surpass General Motors as the most profitable American manufacturer of automobiles. A leading property and casualty insurance company demonstrated the success of total quality through its ability to retain customers and maintain an underwriting profit. A division of a large firm engaged in government contracting demonstrated the success of total quality in part by a win rate on proposals exceeding that of its competitive benchmark and in part through a return on equity that exceeded the industry benchmark.

The point of this discussion is that there is no fixed set of metrics that can be applied to determine whether total quality is successful. The success of total quality cannot be separated from the success that an organization has in accomplishing its purpose. Total quality is a philosophy, a business strategy, a culture change, and a management process. To determine whether such a comprehensive effort is working, it is necessary to make such a judgment from the perspective of the total organization, not just of specific process improvements.

Why Do Universities and Colleges Introduce Total Quality?

Colleges and universities today are under increasing pressure as a result of both external and internal forces. The environment is changing rapidly, and higher education finds that its management structure and its culture make change very difficult. Nevertheless, the forces are creating change in institutions at an unprecedented pace. A growing number of colleges and universities are embracing total quality for the same reasons that led industry and government to embrace it: Existing management systems are outmoded and can no longer ensure success in an increasingly competitive world.

External Forces for Change. The most acute pressure facing public colleges and universities is a reduction in the public funds received or in the rate at which the funds received increase. At a time when higher education correctly argues that society needs its product more than ever, funding has leveled off or is declining. If we look to the future, the projection is that the gap will widen between what higher education will need to perform the role expected of it and the resources that can reasonably be forecast to be available.

As funding declines, higher education organizations have fewer dollars available to reward staff and faculty, adjunct and support staff are reduced, and pressure for heavier course loads increases. This situation leads to difficulties in recruiting outstanding new faculty, especially at public institutions, and to problems in retaining existing faculty in fields where there are employment options. Competition for faculty thus becomes a second external force for change.

Competition for students is a third. Not only initial recruitment but student retention is increasingly important to colleges and universities. One major state university that was underenrolled by approximately 1,500 students in 1993 suffered a loss of approximately $5 million in revenue to the campus. This revenue loss exacerbates a funding situation that was already austere due to several years of reductions in state funding.

As this example illustrates, competition for students is not only a short-term economic issue but also a long-term educational and economic issue. The institutions that attract the best entering students will tend to produce the most successful graduates. If those graduates have a good experience, they are likely to maintain strong ties to their alma mater, from which it reasonable to expect increased student referrals, active participation in alumni associations, and increased giving to the campus. To the extent that total quality can enhance educational and life experience for students, it can have long- as well as short-term dividends.

As institutions of higher education attempt to cope with public funding reductions, pressure to seek funds elsewhere increases. Corporate giving, grants and contracts, personal giving, foundation funds, and fee-generating services are all emphasized. However, donors increasingly require their funds to be traceable. Funds tend to come with strings attached, and funders expect recipients to be accountable. Some funders, especially corporate funders, may explicitly ask an institution to discuss its quality management process as a condition for the receipt of funds. Institutions with a total quality process will have measurement systems in place that enable them to track performance and communicate with funding agencies regarding the performance impact of their contributions.

When a university president makes a fund-raising call on a corporate fund-raising target, he or she commonly describes a range of campus initiatives that may appeal to corporate leadership. The first time the president sees a potential funder's eyes light up at the mention of total quality, the president learns that he or she had better understand what total quality is all about. Such an experience has prompted more than one university president to initiate a quality management or continuous improvement program. Increasing the institution's ability to compete for private funding is a strong incentive for total quality initiatives on campus. However, such an incentive may tempt campus leaders to look for an easy approach simply so they can say that the institution has a total quality process under way. Most corporate funders will be able to see through an effort that is superficial. In the long run, only those campus leaders who have a serious commitment will be able to sustain total quality as a fund-raising advantage.

The last set of external pressures comes from employers. Increasingly, employers are expressing a preference for entry-level employees who have a basic understanding of total quality principles, who can function effectively in cross-functional teams, and who understand the tools and techniques of process improvement. Such employer preferences encourage institutions of higher education to integrate such knowledge and skills into their curricula.

Internal Forces for Change. While the external forces give rise to internal pressures, there are other internal forces that have momentum of their own. Reduced funding creates pressure to reduce costs within the institution. This pressure stimulates actions to increase the productivity of teaching, administration, and support functions.

Like most institutions in society, institutions of higher education are confronting faculty, staff, and students who want to have more voice in decisions that affect them. The shared governance structures in higher education have traditionally given more empowerment to faculty and staff than employees in government and industry have had. However, as elected officials, corporate funding bodies, and higher education boards assert an interest in the accountability of higher education, many faculty and staff feel that their empowerment has been reduced. This feeling, coupled with the absence of salary increases, a condition that many have endured for several years, hurts morale on campus. At some point, low faculty morale spills over into the classroom, where it produces student dissatisfaction. In addition, cost reductions lead to other problems for students: reduced availability of courses, reduced library hours, and increased tuition, parking, and residence hall fees.

Despite these negative forces, most faculty and most administrators are conscientiously trying to find ways of improving educational outcomes for students. Thus, people are looking at the situation that higher education faces as a serious problem but also as an opportunity. Because the situation is viewed as serious, they have an opportunity to propose and implement changes that would not have been considered in the past. It is clear in most higher education environments that the improvements needed in teaching and campus life will not occur through increased funding. What is needed are innovative ways of using the resources that we already have in ways that allow us to do a better job. This will require new management paradigms, new ways of organizing the work of the campus and its functioning. Total quality provides a framework within which we can develop these new ways of working and living together.

How Should Universities and Colleges Determine Whether Total Quality Is Working?

It is obvious from the preceding discussion that the forces motivating the interest of higher education in total quality are broad and fundamental. As in industry and government, we cannot separate the effectiveness of total quality in academia from the fundamental effectiveness of the institutions themselves. Therein lies the rub. Few institutions of higher education have effective systems for measuring performance. Because of the difficulty in measuring results, higher education measures inputs as surrogates for performance. Thus, campus recruiters are more like to cite the rising Scholastic Aptitude Test scores of entering freshman than the increased competence of graduates as evidence of improved performance. Presidents are more like to boast of increases in the annual giving campaign than of improved student perceptions of the quality of campus life. Our ability to measure inputs is much further advanced than our ability to measure outputs and outcomes.

What can we learn from industry and government that would improve our ability to assess the performance of institutions of higher education? Is it possible to translate the metrics used by industry into metrics that can assess whether total quality is helping higher education to improve its performance?

Financial Measures. Let us consider some financial measures or approaches to financial measures that might improve the ability of administrators of higher education to monitor the success of total quality efforts. It needs to be said that all the metrics proposed here are imperfect. However, a less than perfect measure of a critical performance dimension is better than a very precise measure of relatively trivial aspects of performance. Moreover, once a performance indicator has been introduced, it can be taken as a target for continuous improvement. We should work to improve the performance of our measurement systems continually.

The next two sections discuss two approaches to the development of financially oriented measures. Both of the measures proposed are based on a measure commonly used in industry: value added per employee.

Value Added Per Graduate. While higher education has purposes other than simply preparing individuals for employment, employment is an objective of most graduates. Therefore, one measure of the contribution made by higher education is the economic value added per graduate. Value added is the difference between the wages that an individual could have earned without college and the wages that he or she earns after college. If its total quality process helps the college or university to do a better job, value added per graduate should increase. Obviously, this calculation has to control for economic conditions as well as for the differences between career fields.

There are many possible variations of this metric. For example, one could look at differences in earnings with and without college over a five- or ten-year period or even over a lifetime. Economists will doubtless argue that opportunity costs have to be considered. However, the basic concept is to ask what economic benefit accrued to the graduate as a result of higher education. Entry-level wages may offer a better measure of the employer's view of the economic value contributed by the institution, since differences among students affect that value less than they do wages several years after graduation. Entry-level wages would include the impact not only of the academic system but of such systems as counseling, placement, and development.

Value Lost Per Graduate. Some portion of every entering freshman class will fail to graduate. The difference between the potential and the actual value added of a graduating class could be called the *value lost.* This loss should be calculated per graduate to give an institution a basis for comparison with its peers. In nonfinancial terms, value lost is analogous to the dropout rate. However, a simple count of dropout rates probably masks the economic significance of the problem. It can be argued that every transfer or dropout is an institutional failure. It represents a selection mistake, a preadmission counseling mistake, an orientation mistake, or a teaching-learning system mistake. The value lost is not only the difference between the potential and actual value added of a graduating class but also includes the institutional resources spent on the dropout or transfer student before his or her departure. This metric could also be expanded to account for the cost of underenrollment, since a calculation of the potential value added for a class could be based on the slots available in the entering freshman class. The potential value added for available slots not filled is value lost.

Nonfinancial Measures. Industry increasingly is turning to nonfinancial measures to supplement financial measures as a means of assessing performance. These nonfinancial measures help to expand the family of measures to externally oriented measures as well as to measures that are leading rather than lagging indicators of performance. The next two sections describe some potential nonfinancial measures for higher education.

Customer Value. There is a current debate in higher education over who its customer is. Obviously, there are many customers, and the definition of *customer* depends on which of the many "businesses" of higher education we are discussing: research, service, or teaching and learning. To say that there are many customers is true, but it clouds the issue. In order to make substantial progress in improvement, an institution must be able to answer the question, Who is the primary customer? Harlan Carothers, a leading quality scholar at the University of Tennessee, has suggested one way of answering this question (Carothers, 1993, personal meeting, September 1993.) To determine the primary customer, Carothers suggests that we ask the question in this way: Which customer group, if it did not exist, would remove the need for the institution? Applying this question to higher education leads us to conclude that the student is higher education's primary customer.

If the student is the primary customer, then what are the relevant dimensions of value? The relevant dimensions of value should be those that affect customer behavior. In higher education, we can hypothesize three subsets of variables that relate to three sets of behaviors: initial choice of the institution, the decision to remain in the institution, and the decision to stay engaged and support the institution after graduation. We can develop a separate customer value equation for each set of behaviors. Following Carothers (personal meeting, September 1993), customer value equals what the customer perceives that he or she gets minus what the customer perceives that he or she gives up. This concept of value is broader than the economic definition proposed earlier. It is also important to note that this concept of value is a psychological construct–perceived value, as viewed from the customer's perspective.

Each institution must empirically determine its own set of customer value equations for these sets of behaviors. To illustrate, I can show how the determination of value might operate for one set of behaviors. With respect to the initial choice of the institution, what would the student perceive that he or she will get? The answer might include such variables as these: access to courses, anticipated class size, access to faculty, facilities, social environment, intellectual community, reputation, placement success rate, perceived satisfaction of existing students, campus safety, availability of desired extracurricular activities, assistance with job placement, access to attractions in the nearby community (for example, skiing, theater, research libraries). The second part of the value equation is what the student gives up. This will include tuition costs, living costs, and fees. However, it also includes other, nonfinancial costs, such as travel time, and personal considerations, such as the weekend job back home and separation from family and friends. Presumably, if the perceived value is greater for institution A than it is for institution B, the student will choose institution A.

Similarly, we can develop value equations for the factors affecting the decision to remain in school and the behaviors associated with continued commitment to and involvement with the institution after graduation.

Operational Indicators. As with private sector organizations, institutions of higher education have a wide range of operational indicators that can signal whether the quality process is having an internal impact. Table 2.1 lists sample private sector indicators and some typical corresponding indicators for higher education. This listing is not exhaustive, but it provides some examples of the types of operational indicators that institutions can consider when they evaluate the operational impact of total quality. Many of these indicators can be used at both at the campus and departmental level.

It should be stressed that the indicators selected for an individual institution should be those that are in alignment with the campus strategic direction. Therefore, the indicators shown in Table 2.1 are meant only to suggest a range of potential indicators, not to prescribe the indicators that a campus should use.

Table 2.1. Operational and Employee Indicators

Private Sector Indicator	*Higher Education Indicator*
Customer retention	Graduate rate
Product development cycle time	Number of months needed to launch a new course
Unit cost	Cost per credit hour delivered
Warranty cost	Alumni giving rate
Turnover	Turnover in staff and faculty
Proposal win rate	Percentage of students accepted who enroll
Productivity	A family of productivity ratios (for example, number of applicants/recruiting costs, dollars raised/fund-raising costs)
Innovation	Percentage of courses offered that were introduced in the preceding two years

Concluding Comments

This chapter has discussed many forces that are propelling institutions of higher education to change. A large number of institutions have chosen the total quality process as a management system that helps them to guide and focus the change required. Total quality as a strategic management process should be viewed as a way for the leadership of an institution to accomplish the business of the institution more effectively. Therefore, the success of total quality must be assessed in terms of how well the core business of the institution is being accomplished. Such a determination requires the leadership of the institution to develop a scorecard consisting of institution-wide measures that can be used not only to manage the institution but also to assess the institution's success in achieving total quality. A methodology like the SPMM (Tuttle, 1991) can be used to develop these organization-wide indicators. It is critical for this family of indicators to be comprehensive enough to address the concerns of primary customers (that is, students) as well as the requirements of the institution and its other stakeholders. Only through focusing on outputs and outcomes (for example, customer value) and using these performance measures to link the total quality process with results will institutions of higher education be able to realize the potential benefits that total quality can deliver.

References

Gore, A. *Creating a Government That Works Better and Costs Less: Report of the National Performance Review.* Washington, D.C.: U.S. Government Printing Office, 1993.

Hiam, A. *Does Quality Work? A Review of Relevant Studies.* New York: The Conference Board, 1993.

Hronec, M. *Vital Signs.* New York: AMACOM, 1993.

Jacob, R. "TQM: More Than a Dying Fad?" *Fortune,* Oct. 18, 1993, pp. 66–72.

Kaplan, R., and Norton, D. "The Balanced Scorecard: Measures That Drive Performance." *Harvard Business Review,* 1992, *70* (1), 71–80.

Kaplan, R., and Norton, D. "Putting the Balanced Scorecard to Work." *Harvard Business Review,* 1993, *71* (5), 134–150.

Sink, S., and Tuttle, T. *Planning and Measurement in Your Organization of the Future.* Norcross, Ga.: Industrial Engineering and Management Press, 1989.

Tuttle, T. *Performance Measurement for Public Power Systems.* Washington, D.C.: American Public Power Association, 1991.

Tuttle, T., and Romanowski, J. "Assessing Performance and Productivity in White-Collar Organizations." *National Productivity Review,* 1985, *4* (3), 211–224.

Tuttle, T., and Weaver, C. *Methodology for Generating Efficiency and Effectiveness Measures (MGEEM): A Guide for Air Force Measurement Facilitators.* Brooks Air Force Base, Tex.: Air Force Human Resources Laboratory, 1986.

U.S. General Accounting Office. *U.S. Companies Improve Performance Through Quality Efforts.* Washington D.C.: U.S. General Accounting Office, 1991.

THOMAS C. TUTTLE is director of the Maryland Center for Quality and Productivity, College of Business and Management, University of Maryland, College Park.

The steps taken at El Camino College to measure formally the costs associated with process improvement activities are presented. A case study illustrates the institution's first cost-of-quality model.

A Cost-of-Quality Model at El Camino College

Timothy D. Miller

El Camino College is one of the largest single-campus districts in the nation. It enrolls approximately 25,000 students each semester. During its forty-five-year history, the college has become known locally and nationally for its excellent educational, cultural, and sports activities. During the past five years, the college has been actively implementing its formal quality initiative, which is known as Campus Commitment to Excellence. This initiative has involved, among other things, the training of approximately 350 certificated and classified employees, including managers, staff, and faculty. As a direct result of this training in the principles and methods of total quality, approximately thirty-five process improvement teams have been created. These teams have identified certain processes and improved them with varying degrees of success.

In addition, the college has created the El Camino College Quality Institute. The institute provides fee-based training and consulting services to a wide variety of educational institutions and service companies. On the manufacturing side, the college is a member of the IBM Computer Integrated Manufacturing in Higher Education (IBM/CIMHE) consortium. The college is also the recipient of a major grant from the National Institute of Standards and Technology (NIST) that funds the California Manufacturing Technology Center (CMTC). The college provides technical training to aerospace and other manufacturers through its Center for Applied Competitive Technologies (CACT).

The Need for a Cost-of-Quality Model

Like any institution, the college has experienced ups and downs along its quality path. Throughout this period of organizational transformation, there have been voices of opposition. In particular, faculty members have expressed strong opinions both for and against the college's involvement in total quality. Those speaking against it have cited the lack of evidence to support the benefits claimed. That is, to justify the investment of college resources in the total quality initiative, there needs to be some way of accounting for the benefits and the costs. Moreover, they state that the costs and the benefits (cost savings, revenues generated, or both) need to be defined clearly and measured objectively.

It is clear to everyone that dollars represent a common language. They communicate in a meaningful way to a wide audience. Also, costs as measures of process activities can act as benchmarks against which we can measure the extent to which an improvement has made a positive difference. While some of our teams faltered, others made noticeable improvements in their processes and needed some way of measuring their successes. To measure the dollars saved from the improvements made by successful process improvement teams, the college developed a model.

This cost-of-quality model was developed by the Campus Commitment to Excellence Steering Committee over a six-month period ending in June 1993. The committee is responsible for implementing the college's quality initiative on campus. It organizes and monitors all process improvement teams (PITs), and it plans and provides training on campus as needed.

The committee researched several industrial models, especially one used by a major aerospace firm located near the college. The committee discovered that, if several cost factors that applied only to manufacturing were eliminated, the resulting simplified model could be used by service organizations.

The current pilot model focuses on four major areas found in all cost-of-quality models that the committee reviewed: the costs of training and planning for personnel involved in specific process improvement projects; the costs of implementation (identifying, stabilizing, and modifying a process); the cost of materials associated with process improvement; and the costs of inaction (what it would cost not to change). The committee tried also to measure the benefits (cost savings) resulting from process improvement. Thus, it incorporated a fifth category into the pilot model: process improvement results (savings from actions taken).

Pilot Use of the Model: The Big Payback

The team that pilot tested the El Camino cost-of-quality model focused on conference attendance and reimbursement. For years, the college required people who attended conferences to complete two forms. One form constituted a request to attend the professional conference. Approval authorized the applicant to attend the conference and, after the conference, to submit a request for reimbursement of conference-related expenses. To be reimbursed, the conference attendee completed a separate form.

The team's first effort to improve this process led it to revise both forms. Team members first flowcharted the process and used Pareto analysis to prioritize opportunities for improvement. Then, adopting a customer (that is, user) focus, they eliminated non-value-added activities and streamlined the forms. The team members were empowered to make these changes.

The initial reaction around campus was that procedures for conference attendance and reimbursement certainly were a lot better than they had been before. However, the team did not stop there. Instead, the team members continued to meet to explore ways of making the process even better. Their research uncovered another community college that combined the two forms into one. This external benchmarking created a paradigm shift in the team members. Soon, they revised their process again and combined the request for conference attendance with the request for reimbursement into a single user-friendly form. The new form is easier to prepare and requires less time to process than the old ones. Reimbursements that used to take several weeks or even months now take on average around ten days. Team members are proud of their accomplishments. Conference attendees experience much less frustration with the reimbursement process, which has become more efficient. And the college saves time and dollars.

The team members agreed to use the cost-of-quality model to see if it adequately measured the costs and savings associated with their process improvement activities.

The Cost-of-Quality Model. Exhibit 3.1 shows the El Camino cost-of-quality model. This model represents the first effort by the college to capture process costs adequately. The model is being refined with use, and it will certainly undergo many more revisions. That is the way of continuous improvement.

The model used the following weighted-average salaries for three distinct groups of employees. (The amounts shown represent annual salary divided by 2,080—the number of annual hours worked.)

Group	*Annual*	*Hourly*
Administrators	$80,000	$38.46
Faculty	55,000	26.44
Classified/Support	36,000	17.31

The amounts shown in Exhibit 3.1 represent the initial results compiled by the conference attendance request and reimbursement team, which was affectionately known as The Big Payback.

Preliminary Findings. Undertaking process improvement activities in an organization requires an outlay of funds. Sections I, II, and III capture start-up costs for The Big Payback team. They total $21,285.13. However, the changes introduced by the team had the effect of eliminating several steps, and the overall process was streamlined. The resulting reduction of time on task saved the institution $21,316.68. These first-year cost savings essentially offset the initial outlay of $21,285.13. As shown, the first-year net savings equaled $31.55.

Exhibit 3.1. El Camino College Cost-of-Quality Model

Figure 1

I. TRAINING AND PLANNING COSTS (The cost of training and/or planning related to the quality improvement of processes)					
	TEAM: The Big Payback		For CCE Office Use Only		
DESIGNATION	**TITLE**	**HOURS**	**SALARY/HOUR**	**BENEFITS/HOUR**	**COST**
MANAGEMENT:	Margaret Wilson	92	$22.34	$4.69	$ 2,486.76
	Gloria Dawson	92	$19.29	$4.05	$ 2,147.28
CLASSIFIED:	Maggie Hudson	72	$18.13	$3.81	$ 1,579.68
	Lois Ludwig	72	$14.45	$3.04	$ 1,259.28
	Carolyn Vasquez	72	$18.13	$3.81	$ 1,579.68
CERTIFICATED:	Ken Hayward	60	$27.26	$5.73	$ 1,979.40
	PAGE TOTALS	460			$11,032.08

Figure 2

II. IMPLEMENTATION COSTS

(The cost of implementation, data collection, pilot testing, and monitoring of a process improvement. Should include modifications to and stabilization of a process.)

	Unit or Team Fill In		For CCE Office Use Only		
DESIGNATION	**TITLE**	**HOURS**	**SALARY/HOUR**	**BENEFITS/HOUR**	**COST**
MANAGEMENT:	Gloria Dawson	60	$19.29	$4.05	$1,400.04
	Margaret Wilson	60	$22.34	$4.69	$1,621.80
CLASSIFIED:	Maggie Hudson	70	$18.13	$3.81	$1,535.80
	Lois Ludwig	70	$14.45	$3.04	$1,224.30
	Carolyn Vasquez	70	$18.13	$3.81	$1,535.80
CERTIFICATED:	Ken Hayward	79	$27.26	$5.73	$2,606.21
	PAGE TOTALS	409			$9,923.95

Figure 3

III. MATERIALS AND OTHER COSTS

(The cost of services, supplies, and materials used in developing a process improvement: duplication, video rentals, consultants, travel, conference attendance, etc.)

	Unit or Team Fill In	
DESCRIPTION	**ESTIMATED COSTS**	**TOTAL**
Reproduction Costs: Memos	$ 7.20	$ 7.20
Surveys	$ 4.80	$ 4.80
Final Reports	$ 17.10	$ 17.10
Test Forms	$300.00	$300.00
PAGE TOTALS		$329.10

Figure 4

IV. COSTS OF INACTION: WHAT WOULD IT COST NOT TO CHANGE?
Look at the process you are working on. Who is affected by the process (internally/externally)? Answer the following from that perspective.

Quality Indicators (Fill in only as they apply to your team's activity)	Number	Estimated Materials Cost/Year	Manpower Costs Title	CCE Office Only Hours/Year	Cost/Year
1. Number of Customer Complaints Handled:	100/year	N/A	Administrators	24	$ 923.04
			Certificated	24	$ 634.56
			Staff	96	$ 1,661.76
2. Number of Tasks Reworked:	200/year	N/A	Administrators		
			Certificated	60	$ 1,586.40
			Staff	240	$ 4,154.40
3. Number of Unnecessary Steps: Two Conference Forms	1	$127.00	Administrators	24	$ 923.04
			Certificated	60	$ 1,586.40
Administrative Signature	1		Staff	120	$ 2,077.20
4. Number of Scrapped Tasks or Projects:	N/A		Administrators		
			Certificated		
			Staff		
PAGE TOTALS		$127.00			$13,546.80

Figure 5

V. THE PROCESS IMPROVEMENT RESULTS - SAVINGS AS A RESULT OF ACTION
Look at the process you were working on. What changes have been made a result of process improvements? Answer the following from that perspective.

Quality Indicators (Fill in only as they apply to your team's activity)	Number	Estimated Materials Cost	Manpower Costs Title	CCE Office Only Hours Saved/Year	Cost Saved/Year
1. Reduced Number of Customer Complaints Handled:	90/year		Administrators	24	$ 923.04
			Certificated	240	$ 6,345.60
			Staff	90	$ 1,557.90
2. Reduced Number of Tasks Reworked:	175/year		Administrators		
			Certificated	240	$ 6,345.60
			Staff	90	$ 1,557.90
3. Reduced Number of Unnecessary Steps: a. Eliminated one district form	11 days per form		Administrators	24	$ 923.04
b. Reduced steps in process from 22 to 10			Certificated	60	$ 1,586.40
c. Eliminated an administrative signature			Staff	120	$ 2,077.20
4. Reduced Number of Scrapped Tasks or Projects:			Administrators	N/A	
			Certificated		
			Staff		
PAGE TOTALS					$21,316.68

Figure 6

VI. PROCESS IMPROVEMENT COST SAVINGS
(The manpower and materials costs saved as a result of the process improvement.)

Do Not Write Below
FOR CCE OFFICE USE ONLY

NET SAVINGS TO THE DISTRICT	TOTALS
A. **Process Improvement Savings to the District** (enter costs from Item V)	$ 21,316.68
B. **First Year Training, Planning, Implementation, and Materials Costs** (enter costs from Items I,II, and III)	$ 21,285.13
C. **Net Savings to the District in Year One** (subtract B from A)	$ 31.55
D. **Ongoing Savings to the District** (enter costs from Item V for subsequent years only)	$ To Be Determined
E. **Ongoing Planning, Implementation, and Materials Costs** (Enter Item II and III for subsequent years only)	$ To Be Determined
F. **Net Ongoing Savings to the District in Year Two and Beyond** (subtract E from D)	$ To Be Determined

In future years, the cost of such items as training and planning should decrease. However, the cost savings from streamlining the process will continue, and net savings to the college in subsequent years will be larger than the first-year net savings.

The El Camino College cost-of-quality model presented in this chapter represents an initial draft. Admittedly the model needs more work. However, it does provide some means of measuring in dollars the costs and benefits of some of the college's early process improvement activities.

As expected, embracing a continuous quality improvement initiative has additional costs. However, again as expected, these additional costs seem to have a relatively short payback period, after which time the institution experiences an ongoing net savings from its process improvement activities.

Additional Issues and Considerations

The following topics represent only a partial list of the cost-of-quality issues that require additional attention.

The issues of the validity and reliability of the measurements need to be addressed. Validity is concerned with the questions, Are we measuring what we intend to measure? How can we be sure? Reliability asks, How consistent are the measurements? How much variability is there in the measurement system itself? Without validity, we are measuring something other than the true costs of the process. Without consistency, there can be no comparability from one period to the next. If we cannot be confident that the results are both valid and reliable, they do not help management to make decisions.

Perhaps a cost-of-quality model should be viewed more as a cost-of-what-you-do model. Such a model would simply measure the total cost of a process as it operates today. The cost savings that resulted from process improvements could be determined by comparing these costs for two different time periods (for example, compare the current month with the preceding month or with the same month one year ago).

The model should be generally accepted by all persons whom it affects. All involved constituencies should attain a general consensus that the model is appropriate and useful. Such consensus can best be achieved by actively involving all interested parties in the creation of the model.

The assumptions and presuppositions underlying the model must be well thought out and defensible. It must be made clear that conflicting positions received due consideration and that there were guiding rationales for the positions and assumptions finally adopted when the model was formulated. This is important because the savings that accrue from use of the model will probably be used to justify certain management decisions and actions. As these justifications occur, the model will undergo increased scrutiny and challenge by other groups. Does the model stand on solid ground?

An organization needs to systematize the measurement of cost of quality. Institutions need to create a process that can measure the cost of quality. And they need to improve that process continuously as they would any other. The El Camino College cost-of-quality measurement process needs to undergo continuous improvement.

Most cost-of-quality models assume that the important elements of costs are identifiable, quantifiable, and measurable. We need to remember that the most significant elements of the cost of quality are unknown and not measurable. For example, how can the loss to the institution of an unhappy, frustrated, or bitter employee (an internal customer) be measured? How can we measure the negative impact that stories told by disgruntled external customers have on the institution?

Fortunately, this line of thinking can be reversed. The benefits that accrue to the institution from motivated and energized employees or from customers who were surprised by joy also are unknown and not measurable. Nevertheless, these benefits can be felt in a variety of ways, and everyone in the organization can enjoy them. In the business world, this is called *goodwill.* An organization is said to have goodwill when its performance and operating results (typically as measured by net income) are superior to those of competitors.

Savings in the cost of quality do not always progress in a linear fashion. There are relevant ranges of experience that require different considerations and thus interpretations. For example, during the first phase of an organization's effort to implement process improvements, there are necessarily a variety of start-up costs. These can include the cost of training employees and managers; the cost of organizing and supporting a process improvement team; the cost of research, data collection, and development of internal benchmarks; and the costs involved in creating and sustaining a new organizational culture and climate.

As time goes by, many of these costs tend to decline and then to stabilize. For example, after an appropriate cost-of-quality model has been developed, the costs of ongoing use and improvement level out. The point here is that the greatest expenditures are typically up-front and that the cost savings and benefits are typically downstream. Moreover, these savings can for the most part be expected to continue through the life of the organization. Improving quality in the institution is going to cost more initially, because it is an investment. If this investment is made properly, it yields a much greater payoff.

It might be helpful to acknowledge other models of the cost of quality. Some models classify costs under such headings as costs of prevention, costs of detection (appraisal), costs of internal failures, and costs of external failures. Other models distinguish between visible and hidden costs. Still other models define costs as measurable or unmeasurable.

The loss function is also a very appropriate way to view and measure the cost of quality. The loss function is a mathematical expression of the additional costs incurred by an organization when it does not perform or produce at a specified optimum level of quality. It can also be presented graphically and used as a conceptual model to increase awareness of the economic loss suffered by society at large when institutions do not provide the optimum level of quality in their products or services. The loss function emphasizes the need to improve processes by continuous reduction of variation around a customer-defined optimum level of quality.

The measures of costs and the potential savings are what typically grabs the attention of management. The cost savings are often what management points to as the justification for its decisions and courses of action. While costs should not be the only consideration in organizational management, they are undeniably a major factor in the decision-making process.

TIMOTHY D. MILLER is professor of accounting at El Camino College and coordinator of its Quality Institute.

A family of organizational performance measures is presented to monitor improvements in organizational performance resulting from institutional investments in TQM.

Organizational Performance Measures: The Vital Signs of TQM Investments

Barbara A. Lembcke

A growing number of institutions in higher education are investing in the transformation of traditional management practices adapted from Taylorism after the turn of the century into a new style of leadership known as total quality management (TQM). TQM encourages broad staff participation in problem solving, use of new tools and techniques for process improvement, and relentless focus on meeting or exceeding customer needs. The purpose of transforming current management practices into TQM is to increase organizational performance.

Because institutional investments in TQM are long-term and costly, administrators held accountable for investment decisions must constantly monitor and weigh the returns on investments in TQM. The purpose of this chapter is to present a family of organizational performance measures that enable decision makers to monitor and weigh returns on TQM investments. The discussion begins with an operational definition of administrative organizations as a network of interdependent work processes. Examples from operations in selected enrollment management departments are used to illustrate the connections among elements of the work process. Then organizational performance is operationally defined with six measures. Examples from enrollment management are used to illustrate performance indicators.

Viewing Administrative Organizations as Interdependent Work Processes

The first critical step in the transformation of hierarchical, bureaucratic administrative organizations into high-performing, customer-pleasing, streamlined service providers has three parts: clarify customers and understand their needs, expectations, and requirements; clarify organizational purpose; and view administrative tasks called *work* within the context of a network of interconnected, interdependent work processes designed to meet or exceed customer needs.

Clarifying customers and understanding their needs, expectations, and requirements are critical for maintaining customer-oriented service. For administrative organizations engaged in enrollment management, the customer base is relatively clear. The primary customers are students and faculty who directly receive products, services, and information from enrollment management departments. Other external customers are state and federal agencies, lending institutions, and educational systems (K–12, transfer, and graduate institutions). The internal customers of enrollment management departments are all the people and offices throughout the institution who affect or are affected by operations within enrollment management.

Clarifying organizational purpose is critical for achieving and sustaining alignment of critical operational systems. Ambiguity and inconstancy of purpose are the enemies of high-performing organizations. Intended outcomes of organizations, such as goals (in strategic plans) or results (in program mandates), are representations of organizational purpose.

Like most administrative operations in higher education, the administrative units engaged in enrollment management are linked through an interdependent network in which one unit, such as recruitment and admission of new students in the admissions office, supplies critical information, products, or services to downstream operations, such as orientation, registration, and academic advising. The performance of one unit depends largely on the performance of other units upstream that supply it with critical inputs.

According to Sink and Tuttle (1989), organizational systems receive inputs from upstream systems, to which they add value through transformation processes by creating outputs necessary for downstream systems or for meeting customer needs, all for the purpose of achieving specific outcomes. The paragraphs that follow explain these interdependent elements.

Process Outputs and Downstream Systems. Process outputs are products, services, information, or combinations thereof delivered by work processes that serve the needs of downstream systems (internal customers) or external customers. Outputs are designed not only to meet or exceed customer needs but to achieve specific outcomes. Figure 4.1 shows some process outputs (column 2) for departments engaged in enrollment management: admissions decisions for the admissions office; term class schedules, class sheets, and transcripts for the registrar's office; and financial aid award packages for the financial aid office.

Downstream systems are work processes that receive the outputs of upstream systems as inputs. Column 3 of Figure 4.1 shows some downstream systems within enrollment management: commencement planning processes, graduate school admissions, and billing processes for the registrar's office;

Figure 4.1. Process Outputs, Outcomes, and Downstream Systems

(1) *Department*	(2) Process *Outputs*	(3) Downstream Systems *(Internal Customers)*	(4) Outcomes *(Department Level)*	(5) Outcomes *(General)*
Admissions Office	Admissions decisions and notification documents	Registration, orientation, and financial aid award packaging processes	Meeting new student enrollment targets with highly qualified students	
Registrar's Office	Term class schedules, individual student class sheets, transcripts, grade reports, diplomas, graduation lists	Commencement planning processes, graduate school admissions, and billing processes	Filling seats to match enrollment FTE targets	Achieving and sustaining optimal fit between students and the mission and resources of the institution
Financial Aid Office	Financial aid award packages and notification documents	Billing processes and federal auditing processes	Awarding financial aid to all eligible students; achieving targets of total dollars awarded	

Figure 4.2. Upstream Systems and Process Inputs

Upstream Systems	*Process Inputs*
Most Departments	
Faculty and staff hiring and selection processes	Department faculty and staff FTE
Institutional planning and budgeting processes	Department operating budgets; monthly budget reports
Institutional procurement and vendor selection processes	Equipment and supplies
Enrollment Management Departments	
Academic course scheduling	Courses to offer; seats available (registrar's office)
Faculty grading systems	Student grades (registrar's office)
Federal student aid program planning	Aid program guidelines and regulations (financial aid office)
Educational testing services	Names, addresses, and scores of seniors (admissions office)

registration, orientation, and financial aid award packaging for the admissions office; billing processes and federal auditing processes for the financial aid office.

Outcomes. Outcomes are the goals or results that organizations try to achieve. Both intended and unintended outcomes are the result of customers' receiving or experiencing process outputs (products, services, and information). Column 4 of Figure 4.1 shows some department-specific intended outcomes for enrollment management: meeting new-student enrollment targets with highly qualified students, filling seats to match enrollment targets, and awarding financial aid to all eligible students. Column 5 of Figure 4.1 shows some intended outcomes for enrollment management in general: for example, "achieving and sustaining an optimal fit between students and the mission and resources of the institution"—an outcome stated recently by a large, public university.

Upstream Systems and Process Inputs. From upstream systems, work processes receive such inputs as information, materials, trained staff, budgets, policies, and equipment and the other resources that they need to perform their functions. Administrators must keep vigilant watch over the quality of the inputs that support their work processes. Quality control data about process inputs help administrators to determine how well upstream systems are serving and supporting their organizations.

Figure 4.2 shows process inputs for two general classes of upstream systems: systems that serve most departments, such as faculty and staff hiring and selection and institutional planning and budgeting, and systems that service specific departments, such as academic course scheduling, which supplies the registrar's office with courses and seats, and educational testing services, which supply the admissions office with the names, addresses, and test scores of graduating seniors.

Transformation Processes. Work processes convert inputs into outputs through value-added actions that make up the transformation process. On process flowcharts, managers diagram the sequence of work actions that transform inputs to outputs in hopes of discovering and eliminating wasteful work actions that add no value. A thorough knowledge of process work flow enables managers to make informed decisions about future process improvement investments that will streamline operations, reduce nonconformance to standards, or both. Figure 4.3 shows some transformation processes in enrollment management. These processes include the recruiting of students, the processing of applications, the admitting and testing of students, the registering of students, the preparation and sending of transcripts and grade reports, and the advising and counseling of students.

Figure 4.4 illustrates connections among process elements, which are represented by boxes. Process elements begin with upstream systems, which provide inputs to transformation processes that add value in creating or providing outputs that meet the needs of downstream systems and/or external customers, all for the purpose of achieving outcomes.

Figure 4.3. Transformation Processes

Recruiting students; processing student applications; admitting students; testing students (admissions office)

Registering students; preparing and sending transcripts and grade reports; clearing graduation requests; producing and distributing diplomas (registrar's office)

Advising and counseling students; teaching study skills and time management (academic advising and counseling)

Processing aid applications; awarding aid packages and notifying students; advising and counseling students on debt management (financial aid)

Figure 4.4. Work Process Elements and Organizational Performance Measures

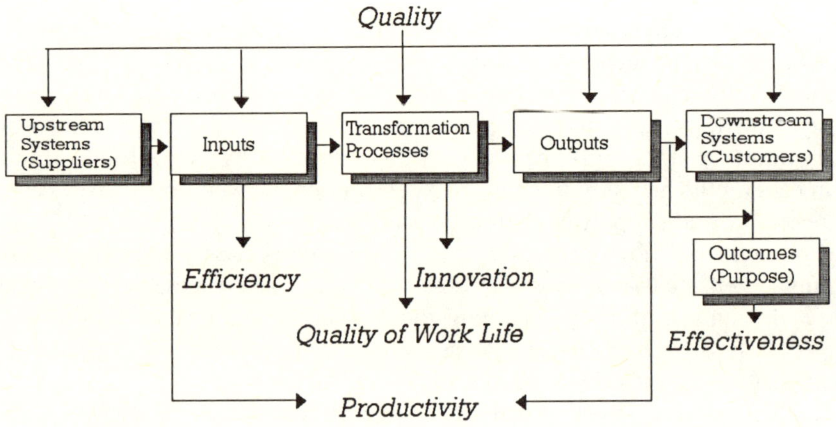

Source: Adapted from Sink and Tuttle, 1989.

Measuring Organizational Performance

Figures 4.1, 4.2, and 4.3 illustrate how work is performed and how processes interact with and depend on one another. They do not explain how well work is performed—in other words, how productive and efficient enrollment management operations are, how much of the work does not add value, how often mistakes are made, how convenient services are for students and faculty, or how enrollment management services and products contribute to optimal fit. All these questions are issues of organizational performance.

In order to measure organizational performance, we must define organizational performance operationally. Sink and Tuttle (1989) suggest a family of performance measures that measure an organization's effectiveness, productivity, efficiency, quality, quality of work life, and innovation. Figure 4.4 relates these performance measures (in italics) to elements of work processes (in boxes.) The sections that follow explain these six performance measures. Figures 4.5 through 4.10 illustrate with examples drawn from enrollment management.

Effectiveness Measures. The most important performance measure of any operation is the one that determines how well it achieves its goals (as in strategic plans) or intended results (as in program mandates.) Data on achievement of outcomes are indicators of the effectiveness of organizational performance.

Department managers in enrollment management services measure their department's effectiveness by evaluating the contribution that its services, products, and information make to optimal fit. (We will assume that optimal fit is defined in the institution's vision and mission statements.) Clearly, department managers must fully understand their department's purpose or desired outcomes in order to measure overall effectiveness. If they do not, any returns on specific TQM investments designed to improve effectiveness may be largely invisible to them and therefore nearly impossible to measure and evaluate.

Figure 4.5 shows some organizational performance indicators of effectiveness in enrollment management. There are four general indicators. They include complaints from faculty about unprepared students, too few or the wrong mix of students enrolled to meet financial targets, and students not enrolled in desired and required courses because too few or the wrong courses were scheduled. The department-specific indicators of effectiveness include the admissions office's yield rate (the percentage of accepted students who choose to enroll), the number of filled seats over or under student full-time-equivalent (FTE) targets for the registrar's office, and the number of students receiving financial aid as a percentage of total eligible students for the financial aid office.

Productivity Measures. Measures of effectiveness do not tell department managers how productive their departments are. To measure this aspect of

Figure 4.5. Organizational Performance Indicators of Effectiveness

Examples for Enrollment Management in General

Faculty complaints about unprepared students

Too few or the wrong mix of students enrolled to meet financial targets

Students not enrolled in desired and required courses because too few or the wrong courses were scheduled

Unanticipated distribution of matriculated student course enrollments by undergraduate/graduate/professional level, by upper/lower division, by discipline area, by in-state/out-of-state

Department-Specific Examples

Number of student accepts as percent of total students admitted (admissions office)

Number of filled seats over or under student FTE targets (registrar's office)

Number of eligible students receiving financial aid as a percentage of total eligible students

Dollars awarded as a percentage of total aid dollars available (financial aid office)

Figure 4.6. Organizational Performance Indicators of Productivity

Number of class sheets, transcripts, grade reports, and diplomas prepared per department staff FTE or operating costs or department computer costs (registrar's office)

Number of students counseled or advised per department staff FTE or operating costs (academic advising center, counseling center, career development center, or student health service)

Number of financial aid award packages prepared per total department staff FTE or department costs (financial aid office)

Number of students recruited per recruitment staff FTE (admissions office)

organizational performance, they need productivity measures. Productivity measures compare process inputs, such as department FTE or operating costs, with process outputs, such as number of transcripts, grade reports, or financial aid award packages prepared and sent. Generally, productivity is easier to measure in transactional operations, such as those that take place in the registrar's office or the financial aid office, than it is in operations, such as student services, that produce one-time programs and events, such as orientation and welcome week.

Figure 4.6 shows some productivity indicators for departments within enrollment management. These measures include number of class sheets, transcripts, grade reports, and diplomas prepared per department FTE or department costs; number of financial aid award packages prepared per total department operating costs; and number of students recruited per recruitment staff FTE. Returns on TQM investments specifically designed to increase productivity in enrollment management are measured by comparing productivity ratios before and after improvement efforts are implemented.

Efficiency Measures. According to Sink and Tuttle (1989), efficiency is a measure of resource allocation and resource utilization. In contrast to productivity, which compares inputs with outputs, efficiency is the ratio of inputs to inputs or of inputs to types of activities and functions. Figure 4.7 shows some efficiency indicators for departments within enrollment management. These indicators include administrative costs as a percentage of total program costs; the difference between budgeted (projected) costs and actual expenditures; and classroom utilization rates. It is important to note that, as work processes become more streamlined, efficiency and productivity will increase, but effectiveness may or may not increase. Returns on TQM investments designed specifically to increase efficiency are measured by comparing efficiency ratios before and after improvement efforts are implemented.

Quality Measures. Effectiveness, productivity, and efficiency are familiar measures of organizational performance in higher education. Quality is a relatively new addition to the family of performance measures. Quality is an important new dimension of organizational performance that differentiates the efficiency, productivity, and costs of value-added work from non-value-added work. Quality measures also address organizational performance from the

Figure 4.7. Organizational Performance Indicators of Efficiency

Administrative costs as a percentage of total program costs
Personnel costs, or current expense costs, or computer costs as a percentage of total costs
Difference between budgeted (projected) costs and actual expenditures
Difference between revenues and expenditures
Distribution of revenues by source
Distribution of expenditures by type
Classroom utilization rates

perspective of customers. How well do outputs meet or exceed their needs, expectations, and requirements?

Figure 4.8 shows some quality indicators for a single department within enrollment management, the registrar's office. Note that quality indicators address all elements of the work process ranging from upstream systems to downstream systems. Returns on TQM investments designed specifically to improve quality can be measured by comparing quality indicator data before and after improvement efforts are implemented.

Quality indicator data are collected through a variety of activities. The next three sections describe several common data collection activities used to increase a department manager's understanding of changing levels of customer satisfaction; reasons underlying customer attrition; the frequency and the causes of underlying variation, such as delays, mistakes, and omissions in the products, services, and information received or provided; and costs of quality, including the costs of poor quality.

Customer Research. At least three data collection activities are necessary if we are to monitor customer perception of organizational performance: customer needs, expectations, and requirements; customer satisfaction or dissatisfaction; and customer loyalty or attrition.

The purpose of assessing customer needs, expectations, and requirements is to establish output standards against which we can measure the quality of conformance. Generally speaking, the customers of support services in enrollment management are students and faculty. They expect prompt, convenient, courteous, and low-cost service; current information; and accurate record keeping. For example, students expect notifications, transcripts, grades, and diplomas to be sent to the correct address the first time, as soon as possible, with no mistakes. They also expect instructions, forms, and procedures to be clear and simple. Everyone expects prompt, courteous, and reliable service when he or she visits or telephones an office.

The purpose of customer research is to understand the degree of and reasons for customers' satisfaction (or dissatisfaction) with the services and products received so improvements can be made. Customer satisfaction research, which is performed after the fact, reveals the gap between customer needs or expectations and customer perceptions. Data explaining customer dissatisfaction are used to add, eliminate, or redesign services and products and to

Figure 4.8. Organizational Performance Indicators of Quality

(1) *Upstream Systems*	(2) *Process Inputs*	(3) *Transformation Processes*	(4) *Process Outputs*	(5) *Downstream Systems*
Costs to verify incoming materials and information from students, faculty, admissions, financial aid, and others	*People:* Number of mistakes from poor training	*Value-Added Actions:* Average turnaround time to process and mail grade reports, transcripts, diplomas, enrollment verifications, graduation requests, and transcript evaluations	*Services:* Average wait time for students to register, to be served at information desks, and to receive transcripts, graduation clearance notices, and enrollment verifications	Number of student, faculty, and staff complaints about services received
	Machines and facilities: Costs of computer down time and equipment repairs			Number of transcripts lost or received late by graduate schools, potential employers, and licensing examination boards
	Information: Number of inaccurate class schedules received from faculty	*Non-Value-Added Actions:* Costs to duplicate services in departments resulting from poor services, reregister students, change grades, drop and add courses, reverse academic actions, republish course schedules, and process domicile appeals	*Products:* Number of inaccurate or missing permanent records, transcripts, grade sheets, student class schedules, graduation lists, and costs of returned mail	Cost of verifying the accuracy of grade reports, diplomas, transcripts, and graduation lists
	Costs of correcting forms received from students with incorrect names, addresses, and social security numbers			

improve processes in ways that decrease nonconformance to standards (errors, omissions, and delays) in the services and products provided. Customer satisfaction data help department managers to determine future quality improvement needs as well as to monitor the improvements in customer satisfaction expected to result from past investments in TQM.

Column 5 in Figure 4.8 shows one quality performance indicator of customer satisfaction: the number of student, faculty, and staff complaints about products and services received. This number represents the gap between expectations that services and products from the registrar's office will be accurate, convenient, timely, and low in cost and perceptions of the products and services actually received.

The purpose of customer loyalty research is to understand which customers did not return for services or products and why. In contrast to customer satisfaction assessment, which is conducted soon after customers receive services or products, customer loyalty assessment is conducted on "disloyal" customers to determine why they did not return. Like customer satisfaction data, customer loyalty data are used to add, eliminate, or redesign services and products and to reduce nonconformance to standards (errors, omissions, and lateness) in the services and products provided. The purpose of customer loyalty assessment is not necessarily to recover lost customers but to learn how to improve services and products in ways that prevent further attrition. This assessment is particularly useful for understanding the issues that underlie increases in the number of nonreturning students, nonrepeat donors, and students defections from residence halls. Data are also useful in explaining why services are threatened by outsourcing or why services are duplicated internally because downstream systems are dissatisfied with official upstream services.

In enrollment management services, students generally have no other choice but to go to the registrar's office if they want to register or to the financial aid office if they seek financial aid. However, dissatisfied internal customers other than students can often go elsewhere for services (such as outsourcing) or have needed services performed within their own department in what becomes a costly duplicate service. In Figure 4.8, customer loyalty data under "non-value-added actions," in column 3, are expressed indirectly as the cost of services duplicated in departments, schools, and colleges because the recipients are dissatisfied with the service provided by the registrar's office. Like customer satisfaction data, customer loyalty data help managers to determine the need for future quality improvement investments and to monitor reductions in attrition or duplication of services expected from previous TQM investments.

Quality Control Activities. The purpose of quality control activities is to measure the degree to which the services and products provided and received do not conform to standards. Most quality control activities are performed by computers and staff who monitor variation in inputs received at the beginning of work processes, as value is added during transformation processes, and in outputs at the end of work processes. The goal is to prevent defective services and products from reaching downstream systems or external customers. Quality control data are usually collected through manual inspection performed by staff or collected electronically through so-called edit or exception reports. Department managers make continuous use of quality control data to monitor changes in organizational performance.

Figure 4.8 shows quality control indicators illustrated for inputs (column 2), transformation processes (column 3), outputs (column 4), and downstream systems (column 5). The input indicators include the number of inaccurate or missing class schedules and grade sheets received from faculty. The transformation processes indicators include average turnaround time to process and mail grade reports and transcripts. The output indicators include students' average wait to register and the number of inaccurate or missing permanent records and transcripts. The indicators for downstream systems include the number of transcripts received late by graduate admissions offices.

Costs of Quality. The purpose of collecting quality cost data is to determine the cost of improving quality and of maintaining current levels of quality. Like other costs, the costs of quality should be budgeted, measured, and analyzed. Cost-of-quality data are critical when the costs and benefits of investments in process improvement must be compared with the costs and benefits of maintaining current levels of quality or of doing nothing at all.

Quality cost data include the cost of work that does not add value (mistakes have to be corrected or the work has to be done all over again); the costs of paying penalties and late fines or of losing the benefit of discounts; the costs of inspecting incoming information, supplies, and equipment, verifying data entry activities in transformation process steps, or proofreading finished products, such as documents and reports, for mistakes and omissions; the costs of auditing operations, litigating cases, or administering grievance and other appeals processes; and the costs of developing and implementing TQM efforts, which include the time spent in training, team meetings, collecting and analyzing data, benchmarking, and managing quality.

Figure 4.8 shows some quality costs for a registrar's office. The costs for upstream systems (column 1) include the cost of verifying incoming materials and information; for inputs (column 2), the costs of computer down time and of time spent correcting forms from students received with incorrect names, addresses, and social security numbers; for transformation processes (column 3), the costs of such non-value-added actions as reregistering students, changing grades, or dropping and adding courses; for outputs (column 4), the costs of returned mail; and for downstream systems (column 5), the cost of verifying the accuracy of grade reports, diplomas, transcripts, and graduation lists.

Quality of Work Life Measures. Quality of work life is a measure of the affective response of members of the workforce to their work life. According to Sink and Tuttle (1989, p. 183), there is a "complex and important link between quality of work life and performance of an organizational system." Figure 4.9 shows some organizational performance indicators of quality of

Figure 4.9. Organizational Performance Indicators of Quality of Work Life

Workforce	*Workplace*
Employee turnover rate	Number of workmen's compensation claims
Employee absentee rate	Number of employee complaints about work environment issues
Number of employee grievance hearings	Organizational climate survey results explaining employee attitudes toward leadership and working conditions
Number of lawsuits	Employee complaints about compensation and benefits packages

work life in enrollment management. Workforce indicators include employee turnover and absentee rates and number of employee grievance hearings. Workplace indicators include number of workmen's compensation claims filed and number of employee complaints about work environments.

Innovation Measures. Sink and Tuttle's (1989) view of organizational performance measures is not limited to quantifiable measures. Thus, they propose innovation as a performance measure. Innovation measures an organization's ability to change its structure, technology, products, products, services, policies, and so on to respond successfully to internal and external pressures and challenges. Figure 4.10 shows some examples of recent creative changes in a registrar's office. These changes include telephone registration, multiple transcripts based on user information needs, and elimination of student transcript fees.

Summary

Those who manage administrative organizations in higher education must view work as part of a network of interconnected and interdependent work processes. Work is not performed vertically through a bureaucratic chain of command but through a series of interconnected work elements designed to produce outputs that meet or exceed customer needs. In order to measure returns on TQM investments, managers must define organizational performance operationally. This chapter has described a family of six organizational performance measures. These measures enable managers to locate and monitor persistent quality problems, allocate resources to improve quality, and—most important—weigh the value of the services, products, and information that customers receive in relation to the achievement of organizational goals and intended results.

Clearly, managers cannot evaluate the return on investments in TQM without a thorough knowledge of organizational performance before and after investment decisions are implemented.

Figure 4.10. Organizational Performance Indicators of Innovation

Organization and Staffing	*Services and Products*	*Policies*	*Technology*
Leadership position expanded from director of student records to registrar	Introduction of a new registration and grade retrieval service using telephones	Incorporation of transcript fees into general student fees to eliminate collection and processing costs	Migration to a new computer
New position called *associate* registrar added	Introduction of a new student developmental transcript to capture nonclassroom learning achievements	Removal of stop flags on student records with outstanding student fees that are less than $5	Installation of new integrated software
Cross-functional process improvement teams created and trained in problem-solving tools	Addition of a new automated degree auditing service that students and staff can use in academic planning	Clarified academic policies that reduce the number of unnecessary student appeals	Development of an electronic transcript transfer system
Staff trained cross-functionally so they can be temporarily reassigned to another section as workload demands shift	Introduction of three types of academic transcripts for students and staff depending on their information needs (internal, official, or unofficial)	Creation of an academic calendar with a new intersession to increase enrollments and shift demand	Creation of induced courseload matrixes for academic planning

Reference

Sink, S., and Tuttle, T. *Planning and Measurement in Your Organization of the Future.* Norcross, Ga.: Industrial Engineering and Management Press, 1989.

BARBARA A. LEMBCKE is senior planning and policy analyst in the Office of Institutional Planning and Research at George Mason University, Fairfax, Virginia.

Total quality management can reduce costs, increase employee involvement, change an institution's culture, and add intrinsic value to the education received by each student.

Value-Added Education: A President's Perspective

Linda M. Thor

Total quality management (TQM) has been called a fad, a repackaging of old ideas, not relevant to education, and an approach appropriate only for businesses and corporations. At Rio Salado Community College, we challenge these claims.

Quality management principles and quality tools are providing Rio Salado Community College with the framework for collaborative planning and decision making that involves students, faculty, administrators, staff, and the community. We use TQM as a methodology for rethinking all the processes associated with higher education. Classroom pilot projects give many students an opportunity to observe or participate in a TQM educational and work environment. We believe that the student experience with TQM is a value-added part of our end product: a student's education.

We cannot entirely quantify that end product other than by counting the number of students persevering, completing their course work, or receiving their certificate or degree. But we can delineate the positive return on our investment of time, energy, and money to implement TQM throughout our organization. Whether or not TQM is a fad, we know that we are better off now as an institution of higher learning than we were three years ago when we introduced TQM into our system, and five years from now we will be better off than we are today because of our commitment to TQM principles and processes.

There is no question that the implementation of TQM continues to require a significant investment of time and human resources on the part of our college, but we find that the improvement in our college culture and in our ability to produce high-quality educational services is significant.

Tangible Results Produced Through TQM

We at Rio Salado Community College have committed ourselves to quality and continuous improvement in our administrative offices and in our classrooms. Since we began our TQM journey in March 1991, we have invested considerable time and effort in bringing about major changes in our culture and in the way that we do business. All regular full-time employees of the college completed a forty-hour basic TQM training. In fact, the average employee has already participated in some eighty-eight hours of TQM-related training, including twenty hours of customer service training and sessions on such topics as giving and receiving feedback, stages of change, and driving out fear. One hundred percent of the full-time employees have served on a continuous improvement team or been involved in the quality initiative.

This investment has produced tangible results that continue to affect our bottom line. Here are just a few of the payoffs: The continuous improvement team revising the process that develops class schedules saved $24,497.73 in printing costs, increased the number of schedules produced by 5 percent, reduced postage costs by $798.13, and cut rework by 28 percent in the first year. These savings are projected to continue each semester that the college schedule is produced. The continuous improvement team addressing student bad debts saved the college $6,504 in the first semester alone by improving the process that instructors use to drop students from the rosters. The annual savings could be as much as $15,000.

On a grander scale, we are particularly proud that a periodic review of our accreditation by the North Central Association of Colleges and Schools in February 1992 granted Rio Salado the maximum reaccreditation of ten years. The review team listed fifteen strengths, including our TQM initiative, and cited only two concerns.

We have developed two new degree programs to meet the growing demands for education and training programs in TQM: one in quality customer service, the other in quality process leadership. And we can state to students and employers that we practice what we preach or, in this case, teach.

Given that when we started our TQM effort, the number one barrier to successful implementation listed by our employees was the district (Rio Salado is one of ten colleges in the Maricopa County Community College District), we are thrilled that the entire college district is now implementing TQM and that Rio Salado's Quality Academy is assisting with the training.

TQM tells us that customer satisfaction is a reflection of employee satisfaction. I am happy to note that our annual survey shows a clear improvement in employee satisfaction since we implemented TQM. When employees were asked in the fall of 1990 to rate the extent to which they felt involved in decisions affecting their jobs on a scale ranging from one (low) to five (high), the average rating was 2.8. Last fall, the average rating was 4.1. And in response to the question, How proud are you to work for Rio Salado? the average rating was 4.5 across all employee groups.

Long-Term Impact

Some of the changes that TQM has brought about have not been dramatically evident. Rio Salado Community College is a college without walls that serves a geographic area the size of the state of Maryland—9,226 square miles. Our 27,000 mostly part-time students (annual headcount) are taught by ten full-time and 750 part-time faculty. Prior to implementation of TQM at Rio Salado, the principal operations of the college were organized in a system of fairly independent, geographically determined offices. We had East Valley, West Valley, Northeast Valley, Central Phoenix, Institute for Culture and Language Learning, and Luke Air Force Base administrative centers.

As the college adopted a structure that was more compatible with quality principles, the system was changed to one that required more interdependence, and areas became functionally rather than geographically defined.

In both systems, the middle managers—associate deans in our system—remain critical to the success both of the college and of the reorganization. In fact, the speed and agility that our college continues to demonstrate in adapting to a quality culture is directly related to the ability of these middle managers to adapt their thinking and styles to our new organizational paradigm.

Two areas of this adaptation in management thinking were especially significant. The first involves the shift from independence to interdependence or, as some would say, from competition to cooperation. The second involves a shift from traditional management to leadership.

In our previous structure, each associate dean in essence ran a minicollege. Together with staff, he or she was responsible for all planning, scheduling, facilities, hiring, payroll, marketing, and so on in his or her area. Each area had its own budget and competed for resources based on its level of student enrollment, which was measured through full-time-student equivalents (FTSEs). This system fostered an entrepreneurial vigor among associate deans, and, like good Americans everywhere, each dean strove constantly to be number one. However, this entrepreneurial spirit also created a fairly high level of mistrust. Useful information was not shared, and unhealthy internal competition among units created divisiveness.

With the shift to a functionally defined system, we have been able to centralize many services, such as faculty hiring, acquisition and maintenance of facilities, marketing, and advertising, that in the past were duplicated. Reorganization made each associate dean responsible for one functional area within the college. The associate deans now have to rely for support on each other. The remaining programmatic operations were grouped in logical academic and occupational functions and assigned to the associate dean most knowledgeable in these functions.

This seemed very reasonable and appropriate to me, and I expected it to be a change that everyone would accept. But however logical the shift from independence to interdependence may have been, it was by no means easy.

After years of making decisions in isolation—of using the informal hierarchy to circumvent the system—managers now had to share information, negotiate for resources, and cohabit in certain facilities.

This new interaction and reliance on others produced many changes. One change involved that most basic of processes, determining the budget. In the past, each associate dean had developed a proposed budget without knowing what the other deans were requesting. Later, in a joint meeting of the associate deans with the dean of instruction (our administrative council), everyone would lay his or her budget on the table, and we would add them all up. As with most budget processes, the total dollars requested usually exceeded the dollars available.

After some discussion and perhaps some argument regarding the figures, senior management took all the proposals, adjusted them as they felt appropriate, and returned them to the associate deans. Any negotiation that took place occurred privately between the individual associate dean and senior management. Such negotiations seldom took place in the open. Often, senior management did not reveal the reasons for the final budget numbers. The assumption was that the numbers would be accepted. As you can imagine, competition and mistrust were rampant.

As the new quality culture evolved, it became evident to everyone that senior management needed to empower middle managers—the associate deans. When that happened, the entire budget process changed.

First, all managers were made aware of the dollars available for all college operations. The associate deans then began a series of working meetings to assess the operating needs of the programmatic areas and the facilities and marketing support that each area required.

Trust accelerated as a result of the openness of the process. The obvious need for give and take among the associate deans enabled them to develop a more effective, cooperative method of working together. While the cooperation began in a less than sincere manner, it soon developed into a true, collegial approach to problem solving.

When the associate deans turned to senior management—that is, to me and my direct staff—and told us that, since they were the people closest to the budget, we needed to trust them with development of the entire budget, it scared us to death. But it worked. The budget that was jointly created by the associate deans came in on target, and the sums available were allocated in a way to which everyone agreed. Not everyone got what he or she had wanted, but everyone agreed to the final product.

Overall, the new management and budgeting structure is more efficient and effective than the old one. This change in our budgeting process is just one illustration of how our total quality culture laid the basis for cooperation and interdependence and produced a better budget as a result, even in times of budget reductions and no growth. Even more important from my perspective as president, the entire process required less time and effort from senior management to reach the desired goal.

Other Changes Brought About by TQM

Our college is changing in many other ways. Every day, we experience a return much greater than our financial investment. We see the human return through increased awareness, expanded empowerment, and broadened horizons.

Our classified employees have increased their self-esteem individually and as a group. The simple fact that we invested time in training all full-time employees sent a critical message to them about their importance in the organization. By placing them on teams with administrators and faculty and removing the barriers and fear that in the past had inhibited intellectual interaction, we have seen individual employees grow to their potential. By asking employees at all levels to make presentations to the governing board, faculty, or deans, we are helping our employees to experience a sense of pride and empowerment that we can see every day.

Through this interaction, we are breaking down barriers that people assumed had always existed in colleges and universities. Employee groups no longer have to be separated in their discussions. Administrators and faculty solve problems together. Staff and faculty share ideas, learn about each other's lives and desires, and work to create an overall environment that enhances the workplace for everyone. The reduction or removal of these artificial barriers has enabled all employees—including faculty members and administrators—to feel more comfortable and secure in the learning environment and to become much more conscious about asking what students need and desire.

Having worked together to develop a vision and refine that vision over the years gives our employees a powerful goal for which to aim. We are not afraid to change our vision, to alter it to meet new challenges, to adjust in light of new ideas, new facts, or changing demographics. Employees know that our vision is alive. We have not placed it on a shelf as we used to do the efficiency reports and consultants' musings. The college vision provides a clarity in the development of strategic goals that everyone clearly understands. And while we have yet to implement some of our goals tactically, everyone understands the direction, because everyone draws passion and emotion from a vision that excites them.

Understanding that students are our primary customer and that their education is our primary product draws ideas and questions from all sectors of our college. People at all levels have developed an insatiable appetite for feedback and for facts and comparisons on which decisions can be based. In the beginning, I must admit, receiving positive and negative feedback on a daily basis from all levels of employees was disconcerting. But it has become commonplace. I do not fear disagreement any more. I see it as a chance to work with those who disagree to reach a common goal to which everyone can commit.

This reduction of fear has led us to some wonderful discussions about critical processes within the college. We cross departmental lines and reduce administrative barriers, and we can concentrate on improving processes without challenging personalities. We have begun to think less about ourselves and more about the impact on students. Our institutional self-esteem has improved, and we are beginning to comprehend what it truly means to be paradigm pioneers.

Decisions Based on Facts

It would be wonderful to be able to say that we only make decisions based on data at Rio Salado, but that would not be true. However, when we do have to make a decision without the proper facts or the statistical framework, we recognize what we are doing. What is different about those decisions is that we now build in a process that enables us to begin collecting the necessary facts so we do not have to make decisions in the future without the supportive data that we need.

We are a long way from benchmarking all critical processes, but we are beginning to break down the informational barriers that we used to impose on ourselves, and we search for benchmarks from private industry and the corporate world. Where we once used the excuse that we were different from private industry, we now recognize that we are similar in many ways.

Our college registers most students by telephone. We can learn from comparisons with American Express or even the Home Shopping Network. We communicate with thousands of potential students by direct mail each year. We can learn from Land's End and United Way. We are attempting to develop benchmarks for the best service delivery, no matter who delivers that service now. Through student surveys and student focus groups, we have begun to concentrate our improvement efforts on where students tell us that we should.

As noted earlier, Rio Salado serves a large geographical area at more than two hundred classroom sites. Most of our students work full- or part-time. Seventy percent of our students take three credit hours or less at any one time. We have to be service oriented. Because we knew that many students could not access our administrative sites during the day, we extended our hours last year into evenings and Saturdays. But data that we gathered on actual student traffic told us that we could meet students' needs by keeping administrative sites open only for the first four Saturdays of each semester. By gathering such data, we saved staff time on nonproductive Saturday hours while we ensured that student needs were met.

The Next Logical Step: The Classroom

For Rio Salado, the next logical step was to take our commitment to TQM directly into our classrooms—not just to teach TQM but to practice it within the classroom setting. If TQM was a method that could improve the productivity of our administrative processes, then it could also be a way to increase student achievement. Rio Salado began TQM initiatives in the classroom in the summer of 1992, approximately eighteen months after TQM was implemented in our administrative units.

The practical applications of TQM in the classroom are based on our commitment to the use of a structured problem-solving process to increase student achievement. Extensive reading and research indicate that educators are using the tools, the process, and the principles, together or separately, to explore ways of improving teaching and learning in individual classes. We decided to begin with that approach, but we have expanded our goals to create a leadership role for Rio Salado in the use of TQM in the classroom.

The first discussions for applying TQM in the classroom came about in the student academic achievement committee. Rio Salado had made a commitment to develop a plan to assess student achievement. We used accreditation requirements to develop an assessment program that flows from our mission. It is based on a conceptual framework, it uses multiple measures for success, it provides students and Rio Salado with feedback, and it leads to continuous improvement. The student academic achievement committee used Rio Salado's quality principles, Rio Salado's principles for quality learning, and the plan-do-check-act cycle to establish Rio Salado's plan for student academic achievement.

Efforts to increase student achievement and improve teaching and learning are occurring in individual courses and in pilot projects throughout the college. Working with the tools and techniques of TQM in large and small discussions, students are able to view the various steps of the learning process. Everyone works toward a common vision and goal. This is constancy of purpose, and it enables even single efforts to have great impact. So, before individual pilot projects were implemented, the student achievement committee brainstormed goals for quality learning and received a great deal of input from the college community. Guidelines and expectations for quality faculty and guidelines and expectations for a quality college were drafted, distributed, discussed, and adopted.

Rio Salado's TQM in the classroom projects keeps the directions and expectations of the college in mind. All these projects have three focus points: curriculum, teaching skills, and learning skills. In each area, a process is analyzed for improvement, and a change is made.

In addition to course- and curriculum-based competencies, the long-term goal is for each Rio Salado student to demonstrate mastery of some general basic and intellectual skills that are assessed separately from those required for courses and majors. Rio Salado has established five goals for quality learning that every general education course is to teach or reinforce. By tracking across multiple sections the required competencies that courses are actually covering, instructors can make any improvements that are needed.

The various TQM pilot projects assess teaching skills in terms of increasing student achievement. An instructor can set goals and collect data regarding specific delivery methods or teaching methodologies to measure their impact on students. Instructors can implement changes that might include use of techniques from accelerated or activated learning, collaborative learning, or teaching to learning styles and measure the effect within the framework of the teaching and learning process and of Rio Salado's goals and direction. One pilot project focused on improving the process of instructional decision making for lesson plans so that instructors could allocate sufficient time for the teaching and learning of course competencies in short-term classes. Instructors find that classroom research tools help them to collect and assess information about their teaching, but the overall framework of the plan-do-check-act cycle is necessary for these efforts to have a significant impact on student achievement.

Students' learning skills can now be assessed, discussed, and improved more readily than ever before. Students are more aware that they are members of a teaching-learning team, and they increasingly become involved in feedback and in assessing their own learning processes. Students involved in one such classroom project at Rio Salado decided to improve their note-taking skills so that they could reduce study time and increase comprehension.

One key factor in the application of TQM principles, tools, and process improvement within the classroom is that each of the three focus areas—curriculum, teaching, and learning—can be initiated either by the instructor or by students. The goal is student achievement, and the instructor and the students are often involved in shared decision making.

Responsibilities at Rio Salado have been clarified. Students and instructors express their needs and expectations openly. The internal standards of the college are delineated. The climate is one of trust and increased participation. The result of practical applications of TQM in Rio Salado's classrooms is increased student achievement within the parameters of its vision, mission, and purposes.

Total quality management at Rio Salado Community College is helping us to develop students who can participate in the management of those processes, who understand quality, and who are skilled in process improvement. Developing applications for TQM in the classroom took time, commitment, and communication, and everyone was involved. But it is producing a generation of Rio Salado students who can overcome the problems that they face in the workplace.

Beginnings

The journey at Rio Salado Community College is well under way. Staff, faculty, administrators, community leaders, and students have already dedicated thousands of hours of work and commitment to this ongoing project. However arduous the effort may be, the basic question remains, Can Rio Salado honestly say that the benefits derived from implementation of TQM outweigh the costs associated with changing paradigms? The answer is clearly and resoundingly yes. Employees are more productive. Budget processes promote appropriate outcomes. The college has saved tens of thousands of dollars from process realignments in areas ranging from printing to student bad debts. We have been invited to participate more openly in the community with local business and industry. But while we see an absolute return from the dollars already invested in total quality, we have not yet completed our investment. In fact, we probably never will. New employees must be trained. Continuing employees must receive more training and be helped to expand their own horizons.

To change the way in which our colleges and universities work and educate people will take a long time. For Rio Salado, I do not know when or even whether the end will come. But I do know that we have begun and that employees and students are benefiting from that beginning. We are no longer the college that we once were. We are not yet the college that we want to be. We are a college dedicated to continuous quality improvement.

LINDA M. THOR is president of Rio Salado Community College, a recipient of the 1993 Arizona Governor's Award for Quality.

Efforts to integrate total quality concepts at the U.S. Air Force Academy have been under way for approximately three years. Several lessons from its experience seem broadly applicable.

The Costs and Consequences of Quality at the Air Force Academy: A Professor's Perspective

David B. Porter

The question of whether quality was worth doing at the U.S. Air Force Academy is not really very interesting. The Air Force Academy never had a choice; quality was mandated by higher headquarters. However, the question of whether doing quality right was worth the authentic commitment that it required is an altogether different and perhaps more important question.

After a brief description of the Air Force Academy and its mission, students, and faculty, I address the question of why quality resonated with so many of the needs of this institution. A description of a simple model that provided a conceptual framework for initial quality education and training activities will be followed by evidence of our progress thus far. Despite the many substantive differences between the academy and other institutions of higher education, the study described in this chapter supports the conclusion that the right kind of investment in quality is well worth the cost.

The Academy and Its Mission

The U.S. Air Force Academy is a four-year undergraduate college. Its stated mission is to develop and inspire air and space leaders with vision for tomorrow—in other words, to provide the nation with commissioned officers for

---

Opinions expressed in this chapter are those of the author and do not necessarily reflect the position of the U.S. Air Force Academy or any other government agency.

military service. Academy cadets (students) are selected competitively, but they do not pay tuition. They incur a commitment to serve for several years of active duty in the Air Force upon graduation. The cadet wing (student body) numbers about four thousand. Approximately 13 percent are women, and 10 percent represent racial minorities. As a group, cadets are very bright (entry Scholastic Aptitude Test scores average near 1,250) and very athletic (more than 80 percent earned a varsity letter in high school), and they tend to share a somewhat conservative and traditional worldview.

The academic faculty is composed of five hundred Air Force officers assigned to nineteen different academic departments. Several Army and Navy officers as well as approximately thirty visiting civilian professors are also part of the faculty. (Recently, the academy began hiring full-time permanent civilian faculty. The goal is to convert approximately 125 faculty military positions by the year 2000.) Most of the military officers newly assigned to the faculty have between six and ten years of military experience and an appropriate master's degree. They serve four-year tours on the faculty, then return to the operational Air Force to continue their military career. Several faculty officers are sponsored for doctoral study and return to the academy for second or third four-year tours. Currently, about 30 percent of the faculty have earned the doctoral degree. Nonetheless, the faculty's average teaching experience is very low—about two years—and turnover is very high—between 20 and 40 percent a year. Strong emphasis on faculty development, small classes (twenty or fewer students in most cases), and a very low student-teacher ratio (eight to one) help to offset the perennial lack of teaching experience.

Why Quality?

In many respects, the mission of the military (and consequently of the academy) has not changed. The preeminent military mission is to prepare for and prevail in combat. However, the nature of combat has changed. This change in turn has had significant consequences for the way in which the academy must develop and inspire its students to become air and space leaders. Technology has increased both the precision and the lethality of our weaponry, military operations have become increasingly complex and interdependent, and chaos has replaced Communism as our principal foe. Military effectiveness in the future will depend far more on flexible and enlightened leadership than it has in the past. Recognition of these new challenges provided a strong impetus for considering new approaches to education at the academy.

Another reason why the quality perspective was so attractive may have been the special relationship between quality and the academy's central purpose, namely leadership. Many of Deming's concepts and principles (1982) contradict much of the prevailing academic literature in management. In contrast, his perspective receives strong support from the interdisciplinary collection of theory, evidence, and anecdote that constitutes leadership studies. In particular, Deming's emphasis on the integration of systems, statistics, psychology, and epistemology resonates with the literature on leadership (Rustow, 1970; Stogdill, 1974; Burns, 1978; Simonton, 1984; Hollander, 1978; Bennis and Nanus, 1985; Hughes, Ginnett, and Curphy, 1993).

In contrast to management, leadership places greater emphasis on the human side of the organization. Because it recognizes holistic and somewhat less tangible aspects of organizations, leadership involves art as well as science. Leadership is not just the study of what leaders do; it is the study of the many complex interactions between leaders, followers, and situational factors in the context of particular goals (Stogdill, 1974; Hughes, Ginnett, and Curphy, 1993). For those seeking a literature that provides a framework for understanding quality, leadership studies are ideal.

Similarities between Deming's fourteen points (1982) and axioms of military leadership have greatly facilitated the adoption and implementation of quality concepts by many military organizations over the last decade. Perhaps it is more than just a coincidence that General Douglas MacArthur was the man who first invited Deming to share his ideas and approach with the Japanese. Statements by military leaders underline this convergence between quality and military values. According to General Merrill McPeak, Air Force chief of staff, "The quality Air Force pushes power down the organization; our people must be able to think and do in order to improve our operations" (U.S. Department of the Air Force, 1993, p. 1). "Be very suspicious of anyone who tries to tell you the quality movement in the Air Force is about management," warns General John Loh, commander of the Air Combat Command. "It's not. It's about leadership, specifically leadership that creates a working climate characterized by trust, teamwork, and a quest for continuous improvement" (U.S. Department of the Air Force, 1993, p. 1). And Lieutenant General Eugene Fischer, Air Force inspector general, defines quality as "a journey that permeates everything you do. It's a way of life, it's a lifestyle, and, most importantly, it involves leadership" (U.S. Department of the Air Force, 1993, p. 1).

How Did We Do It?

Although it might be ideal, persuading everyone in the organization to study leadership is not possible. A common initial need is to find a way to express, in clear and direct terms, the most essential aspects of total quality. Deming's fourteen points make perfect sense to those with experience trying to effect quality changes, but they are much less impressive to the uninitiated. Greater conceptual simplicity is needed.

The quality-mobile developed by Porter (1992a), provides an alternative formulation of several important quality principles. The model depicts an automobile moving forward on a path toward total quality. Understanding and trust are the quality-mobile's two axles. They are equally important. Successful organizational transformation requires synchronized increases in both understanding and trust.

A brief explanation of the model's mechanics will be helpful. We can start with the rear axle. Creating explicit models of an institution's critical processes and then systematically collecting data relevant to them is the way to increase systemic understanding. However, such institutional inquiry will inevitably evoke considerable resistance unless efforts to increase organizational trust—the front axle—are equally effective. The suspicion that leaders are using total quality to impress politicians or alumni will kill any effort to transform an organization before the effort begins. Although a leader's willingness to walk the talk of total quality is necessary for the development of trust, it is not sufficient. Leaders must also consistently convey positive expectations. It is human nature to trust those who trust us. Timing and style are also critical. The particular quality initiatives that are undertaken are less important than when and how they are undertaken.

Institutional integrity is the extent to which policies and programs are consistent with stated goals. Consequently, the behavior and apparent attitudes of institutional leaders are likely to be examined closely. Attempts by leaders to coerce, cajole, or manipulate others are likely to undermine organizational trust and thus inhibit quality. Extensive use of punishments (or even rewards) is almost certain to be counterproductive in the long run (Kohn, 1993). The motivation to do quality work must come from the work itself. In this regard, educators are ideally situated to benefit from the incorporation of quality. Not only were these concepts and considerations the content that needed to be conveyed to the rest of the faculty, they also framed the transformation process.

The rapid development of a quality orientation in the Air Force created external support and validation for educational initiatives that had been under way at the academy for several years. Among these were efforts to enhance cadets' critical thinking skills, the development of collaborative pedagogies, systematic measurement of student satisfaction, and increased interdisciplinary integration and awareness. Educators who participated in these efforts gained valuable experience working together to implement measurable academic improvements.

Quality might be thought of as an institutional virus. Initially, it needs an environment in which concepts extracted from the experience of others can be examined and adapted to the particular needs of the institution. Typically, a small cadre of individuals with a broad institutional perspective provides an ideal host for the nurturing of quality germs.

The applicability and potency of the concepts articulated in such books as Peter Scholtes's *The Team Handbook* (1988), Peter Senge's *The Fifth Discipline* (1990), Rafael Aguayo's *Dr. Deming* (1990), and William Glasser's *The Quality School* (1990) were immediately obvious to those struggling to improve teaching and learning. Attendance at national and regional conferences and conventions facilitated the collection and integration of a great deal of information about the theory and practice of total quality (Porter, 1991). Subsequent informal discussions among members of the small group increased the understanding of how the successes and failures of other educational institutions might be applied to the academy. When interest in the new quality paradigm was expressed by top Air Force Academy leadership, a cohesive cadre of internal experts was ready to serve as a catalyst for organizational change.

Faculty members who visited national conferences returned full of enthusiasm for quality concepts and techniques. Unfortunately, sending each faculty member to a national conference on quality was well beyond the academy's limited budget. It was also clear that many of those unfamiliar with the broader quality literature returned from quality conferences with unrealistic expectations concerning the speed, potency, and simplicity of total quality transformations. Another possible approach was to invite external consultants to provide on-site quality training for the faculty. Unfortunately, initial presentations by external quality experts and consultants generated considerable resistance among other members of the faculty. (Even military educators can be rather intolerant of those without appropriate academic credentials.) It did not take long for us to realize that developing our own unique program was necessary. There were two essential steps: We needed first to clarify our goals, then to secure explicit support from the institution's leadership.

Extensive discussion among the quality cadre led to agreement that our goal would be to create a system that enabled everyone to take pride in his or her work. This effort would necessarily involve not only the faculty and staff but also students. However, unless the institutional leadership was willing to make an authentic commitment, no amount of training would be sufficient even to begin the transformation.

After receiving the external mandate to pursue quality in the fall of 1990, institutional leaders invited the quality cadre to conduct a two-day workshop in the spring of 1991. This workshop made it clear that there was general understanding of and support for an authentic quality transformation at the academy. The next task was to create a comprehensive quality education program.

What Progress Has Been Made?

Much of the 1992–93 academic year was devoted to developing and implementing total quality education and training courses for all academy personnel. Although the Air Force mandated training, it gave us considerable latitude in selecting content and style. The cadre of educators considered it their personal responsibility to develop the best quality curriculum possible. One of the academic department heads, Colonel Richard Hughes, was granted an in-house sabbatical and designated to head the quality development and implementation program. He met with the cadre of educators for approximately two months to plan a curriculum. As soon as the team had a general idea of issues, priorities, and alternatives, the decision was made to test-market the program with prospective customers.

We arranged to conduct a month-long series of seminars for twenty-four other individuals who would serve as trainers for nonacademic personnel stationed at the academy. As the superintendent, Lieutenant General Bradley Hosmer, explained at the initial meeting, their task as quality educators was not to become trained canaries but to understand quality so well that they could enlighten and energize their audiences. These seminars provided the cadre with an opportunity to test their own teaching as well as receive invaluable feedback from some very motivated students of quality. Their practical suggestions and insights consistently led to improvements in the curriculum. By the end of the fall semester, training for nonacademic personnel had begun in earnest, and we could turn our attention back to the thorny problem of how to educate the faculty.

Creating an appreciation among faculty members of the educational and organizational opportunities afforded by total quality is a unique challenge. Faculty members are all expert debaters and persuaders. As such, they can easily become intransigent defenders of traditions that they may themselves have denounced in the past. This is particularly true if they believe that quality is being imposed on them from the top or, worse, from sources outside the hallowed halls of academe. Although the faculty consist mostly of officers who know how to follow orders, the folly of a simpleminded, frontal assault was obvious. Orders can only ensure attainment of minimum standards. Quality requires just the opposite. Everyone must focus on helping to realize an ideal. People must be willing to do their best and give it their all.

Although limitations of space prevent me from including our two-day syllabus for total quality education, several key principles can be noted. Because the medium is the message, considerable effort was made to ensure that the conduct of the workshops reflected our best understanding of the process of learning and the development of trust. Learning occurs in a context. Departments were scheduled together for workshops, and senior officers participated in the planning and conduct of the workshop. The cost of quality should be shared equitably. The dean granted two faculty "down days" for each department to conduct the workshop. Teachers (like their students) often learn more from what they have said than from what they have heard. Sixty percent of the workshop time was allotted to small-group activities and discussions. Another distinctive aspect of the workshops was the extent to which quality concepts and theories were combined with assessment techniques to give participants an opportunity to explore the educational systems within their own departments. Our goal was for faculty members to become comfortable with quality concepts and recognize the opportunities that quality offered for achieving excellence. Although this message was seldom if ever stated explicitly, we consistently sought to convey it throughout each of the twenty-six two-day workshops.

What Have Been the Consequences of Quality?

The return on investment in effecting a quality transformation will accrue at many levels (Porter, 1992c). There are returns at the institutional level in terms of increased commitment, decreased parochialism, and increased interdepartmental communication and cooperation. The entire faculty have benefited from such quality initiatives as the development of a comprehensive course critique program and common educational outcomes that were a direct result of the departmental quality workshops. Not too surprisingly, the greatest benefits are appearing in departments that have been pursuing quality the longest. Increased emphasis on decentralization, diversity, and development contributes to positive shifts in organizational climate and effectiveness at the departmental level. And finally, as Rolf Clark (1992) suggests, the authenticity that individual growth and development require can occur only in an environment where the emphasis has shifted from looking good to doing well.

Faculty. One key institutional activity that served as a harbinger for the introduction of total quality was the adoption of a comprehensive course critique program (Porter, 1988, 1992b). On the assumption that faculty would use direct, objective feedback from students to improve their own performance, this program provided every instructor with ratings from students for each section at the end of each semester. In the first two years of use, average ratings for the whole faculty increased by nearly a full standard deviation. This meant that the rating that an average instructor received in the fall of 1991 would have placed him or her on the 80th percentile just two years earlier when the critique was first introduced.

Another important return on the investment in quality at the faculty level has been the development of a common language for talking about education. Interdepartmental dialogue has led to increased understanding and appreciation of our own academic diversity. To the surprise of many, faculty members have even neared consensus on a set of general educational outcomes. The first outcome concerns the breadth and depth of knowledge that graduates should possess, but the other six reflect important skills and attitudes that our graduates should display. We seek to produce officers who can frame and resolve ill-defined problems, communicate effectively, work effectively with others, and apply their knowledge and skills to the unique tasks of the military profession. Our goal is to graduate officers who are independent learners and intellectually curious. The content of these outcomes is interesting in its own right. Even more important, the process of reaching consensus about these outcomes created institutional momentum for efforts to explore and develop ways of assessing their attainment. What we as faculty learned from the process of engagement and dialogue is one of the most valuable returns on the institution's investment in quality.

This is not to suggest that the all the faculty have become converts to quality. Several departments still frown on outright advocacy of total quality. The extent to which practices and programs actually changed as a result of the workshops varied. Lewin (1958) indicates that organizational change occurs in three distinct stages: unfreezing existing group attitudes, establishing new attitudes, and then refreezing the new attitudes. The purpose of the initial workshops was to help to create an environment in which traditional attitudes and assumptions could begin to thaw. The shift to new perspectives and practices will occur as departments explore the process of education independently and share what they learn with one another.

A Department. The Department of Behavioral Sciences and Leadership is one of the largest at the academy. Total faculty and staff include nearly fifty officers and civilians. Required courses in general psychology and leadership as well as about fifteen elective courses are taught every semester. The academic majors programs offered in human factors and human behavior attract more than a hundred cadets a year. Despite a 50 percent faculty turnover in the past year (due primarily to Air Force personnel inducements toward voluntary separation) and an average teaching experience of less than one and a half years, teaching effectiveness ratings from students remain near the top of the faculty (8.5 on a ten-point scale). Enrollment in the two majors tracks has increased by approximately 20 percent every year for the last three years. Similarly, feedback from the annual organizational climate survey shows that departmental effectiveness, morale, and satisfaction among its faculty and staff have increased consistently and substantially to their highest levels ever. Faculty ratings on a seven-point scale of their own understanding of quality concepts is 6.0 (1.0 SD). On the extent to which individuals are treated with respect, the rating is 6.2 (1.0 SD), and on the overall quality of work, it is 6.4 (0.7 SD).

However, excellence in education is much more than numbers. Departmental commitment to quality has given us the opportunity to improve our understanding of the processes that allow everyone to contribute to the mission of developing and inspiring students. Increased pride in all aspects of scholarship is perhaps the most valuable return on an investment in quality.

Conclusion: Is Quality Worth the Investment?

Contrary to the hackneyed phrase, quality is not free. But neither should quality be so exorbitantly expensive that it necessitates a drastic redistribution of scarce institutional resources. The extraordinary effort that quality requires is unlikely to be secured by providing extrinsic rewards or paying clever quality consultants. Ironically, quality depends most critically on a resource that is already distributed throughout organizations: the potential of individuals to do the kind of work in which they can take pride. Quality gives everyone an opportunity to contribute significantly to the important work of the institution. Once people realize this and appreciate its significance, resource limitations are likely to recede. As Aguayo (1990) suggests, emphasis on quality will almost inevitably increase effectiveness and efficiency, but emphasis on either or both is not likely to improve quality. At the same time, it is not likely that many individuals will risk the level of personal commitment necessary to sustain a quality transformation unless the institution itself makes a clear and unequivocal commitment to quality.

Another way of looking at the concluding question is to consider the alternatives. The world in which we live is neither flat nor still. Things are changing, and so are our competitors. Earlier, I suggested that technology, demography, and politics were changing the nature of warfare. Is this any less true of education? Many of the factors that nurtured and that continue to shape the implementation of quality at the U.S. Air Force Academy are undeniably unique. Likewise, many of the benefits enumerated earlier may be unique artifacts of a particular confluence of military, educational, and quality factors. There are myriad reasons for institutions not to embark on a journey toward quality. However, the most important decisions about quality are those made by individuals. The possibility that quality can become a catalyst for recapturing the energy and optimism that attracted each of us to the academy has made it well worth our investment.

References

Aguayo, R. *Dr. Deming: The American Who Taught the Japanese About Quality.* New York: Carol, 1990.

Bennis, W., and Nanus, B. *Leaders: The Strategies for Taking Charge.* New York: HarperCollins, 1985.

Burns, J. M. *Leadership.* New York: HarperCollins, 1978.

Clark, R. "TQM from the Trenches: The Role of the Individual." *Program Manager,* Mar./Apr. 1992, pp. 28–32.

Deming, W. E. *Out of the Crisis.* Cambridge, Mass.: Center for Advanced Engineering Study, Massachusetts Institute of Technology, 1982.

Glasser, W. *The Quality School: Managing Students Without Coercion.* New York: HarperCollins, 1990.

Hollander, E. P. *Leadership Dynamics: A Practical Guide to Effective Relationships.* New York: Free Press, 1978.

Hughes, R. L., Ginnett, R. C., and Curphy, G. J. *Leadership: Enhancing the Lessons of Experience.* Homewood, Ill.: Irwin, 1993.

Kohn, A. "Why Incentive Plans Cannot Work." *Harvard Business Review,* Sept./Oct. 1993, pp. 54–63.

Lewin, K. "Group Decision and Social Change." In E. E. Maccoby, T. M. Newcomb, and E. L. Hartley (eds.), *Readings in Social Psychology* (3rd ed.). Troy, Mo.: Holt, Rinehart & Winston, 1958.

Porter, D. B. "Course Critiques: What Students Can Tell Us About Educational Efficacy." In *Proceedings of the Human Factors Society 32nd Annual Meeting.* Santa Monica, Calif.: Human Factors Society, 1988.

Porter, D. B. "Total Quality Education." In K. D. Lam, F. D. Watson, and S. R. Schmidt (eds.), *Total Quality: A Textbook of Strategic Quality Leadership and Planning.* Colorado Springs, Colo.: Air Academy Press, 1991.

Porter, D. B. "The Quintessence of Quality." In *Proceedings: Psychology in the Department of Defense—Thirteenth Symposium.* Colorado Springs, Colo.: Department of Behavioral Sciences and Leadership, U.S. Air Force Academy, 1992a.

Porter, D. B. "Student Course Critiques: A Case Study in Total Quality Education." In *Proceedings: Psychology in the Department of Defense—Thirteenth Symposium.* Colorado Springs, Colo.: Department of Behavioral Sciences and Leadership, U.S. Air Force Academy, 1992b.

Porter, D. B. "Total Quality Transformations." In *Mountain Plains Management Conference: Diversity and Complexity as Organizational Assets.* Colorado Springs, Colo.: Department of Management, U.S. Air Force Academy, 1992c.

Rustow, D. A. (ed.). *Philosophers and Kings: Studies in Leadership.* New York: George Braziller,

1970.

Scholtes, P. R. *The Team Handbook: How to Use Teams to Improve Quality*. Madison, Wis.: Joiner Associates, 1988.

Senge, P. M. *The Fifth Discipline: The Art and Practice of the Learning Organization.* New York: Doubleday, 1990.

Simonton, D. K. *Genius, Creativity, and Leadership: Historiometric Inquiries.* Cambridge, Mass.: Harvard University Press, 1984.

Stogdill, R. M. *Handbook of Leadership: A Survey of Theory and Research.* New York: Free Press, 1974.

U.S. Department of the Air Force. *Current Messages for Senior Air Force Leaders.* Washington, D.C.: Office of Public Affairs, Secretary of the Air Force, 1993.

DAVID B. PORTER is professor in the Department of Behavioral Sciences and Leadership, United States Air Force Academy, Colorado.

There is no such thing as a free lunch. University administrators should decide whether the benefit expected from TQM justifies the cost before they join the revolution.

A CFO's Perspective on the Quality Revolution

Alan J. Norton

Traditionally, the chief financial officer (CFO) of a college or university is the gatekeeper or guardian who is responsible for overseeing the proper use of institutional resources. CFOs are cautious, and their judgment is typically that of a prudent person. Statements like these are normally made by trustees and colleagues as part of an eulogy. While CFOs are active, they are often called bean counters or even harsher names if the current shape of the institution's budget seems to warrant it. While some CFOs can gain such a reputation by consistently saying no without even hearing a dean's request for an increased expenditure, most do so by demanding answers to tough questions about the internal rate of return on investments or the value of a new expenditure for the long-term well-being of the university or by pressing divisions, departments, or individual deans to cut costs or increase productivity. What then would be the perspective of a CFO regarding total quality management (TQM)?

One can approach the analysis of TQM from any number of perspectives. A CFO's viewpoint is essentially economic, and the basic notions of economics provide the tools for the analysis. The CFO should ask the questions, How does TQM measure up in terms of opportunity cost? and What are the benefits relative to costs of TQM?

To discuss TQM, one must first be clear on the definition. Deming (1982) is generally accepted as providing the foundation for TQM. In this chapter, the experience of St. John Fisher College in Rochester, New York, will be used to illustrate the costs and benefits of TQM. TQM is the approach to administrative leadership and operations that has evolved at the college since 1988. TQM, which at the college is called *total quality leadership,* is consistent with

Deming's (1982) views. The college's implementation of TQM has been influenced by other writers as well: Mann (1985), Scherkenbach (1986), and Juran (1989) have clarified Deming's (1982) positions and amplified the concepts of TQM. How-to manuals dealing with teams and quality tools (Doyle and Straus, 1976; Scholtes, 1988; Brassard, 1989) have been used at the college. Recent literature (Coate, 1990; Shafer and Coate, 1992; Melan, 1993) related specifically to higher education that describes both general approaches and actual experiences has influenced the college's quality journey. The available published material; training provided by GOAL/QPC, Xerox, Eastman Kodak, and W. Edwards Deming in his famous four-day workshop; and a number of national and regional conferences have all provided background for the implementation of TQM at St. John Fisher College. So, while every organization's implementation of TQM is ultimately unique, one can reasonably generalize from a number of the college's experiences.

While TQM at St. John Fisher College is fairly close to the conceptual model, it has been essentially an administrative experience. A few faculty on campus, ranging from philosophers to organizational theorists, have studied TQM as an academic topic, but only a couple of academic departments have attempted to use TQM as an approach to their academic administration. Similarly, only a couple of faculty have adopted TQM as a framework for the delivery of direct instruction. In addition, one of the conceptual hurdles that educational institutions have to overcome is the dilemma of sorting out the traditional roles of students, faculty, administrators, staff, and trustees as internal and external customers and suppliers. This hurdle is especially difficult relative to the relationship between faculty and students. While it is obvious that the student is a paying customer, the student is also a coworker with faculty in the enterprise of learning. An ideal model of TQM in higher education would have all members of the academic community using its concepts and tools to maximize education and scholarship per dollar spent. While the reality today at St. John Fisher College and elsewhere is far from this ideal, a legitimate consideration of costs and benefits can still be undertaken.

Costs of TQM

The costs associated with TQM relate primarily to organization and training. The relevant costs to consider are the incremental costs associated with the use of TQM. For example, I would not consider the time and energy that a CFO spends learning and doing TQM a cost of TQM unless it results in the need to hire an assistant to do work that is not getting done. Learning about TQM can generally be accomplished within the discretionary time that is part of most exempt jobs. Whether students will someday be familiar with the concepts and tools of TQM when they graduate from high school remains to be seen, since to date only a handful of secondary schools have made TQM a central part of their curriculum (Schargel, 1993; Salmon, 1993). Consequently, the organization that adopts TQM will have to be responsible for the education of its own workforce, and in postsecondary education that means training the student body.

Key Leaders. The primary leader and key secondary leaders of an organization—ideally the president and vice presidents, as at St. John Fisher College—must be fully committed to and involved in TQM. The vice president of a large division at a university can initiate TQM along with the associate vice presidents or key divisional directors, but a great deal of the potential benefit is lost when interdivisional (cross-functional) improvement projects cannot be undertaken. While the primary leader must be personally involved, the primary leader typically delegates some of the implementation work. The experience of St. John Fisher College is that approximately one full-time equivalent (FTE) employee has been needed to organize the training of the two hundred FTE nonfaculty members of the workforce. To organize and implement the training properly, the following skills were needed: expert knowledge of TQM, expertise in the training of employees, and clerical support. While a number of individuals could have all these skills, the law of comparative advantage led the college to spread the one FTE employee over several people. This was done by reallocating the personal discretionary time available to senior administrators and by adding one part-time clerical position. In larger organizations, more than one FTE would be needed, but the human resources department may already have an employee development and training operation that could handle some of this work. Again, the important cost is the incremental cost, which will be less than the total cost of the resources actually devoted to the project, since some are simply reallocated from other efforts to manage the institution.

TQM Expert. Someone needs to become an in-house quality management expert as soon as possible. This individual can be the primary leader, or that person can appoint a special assistant for quality who becomes the institution's first expert. The special assistant should report in this role directly to the primary leader. The primary leader and the special assistant should develop the implementation and training plan along with the training experts and other secondary leaders.

Within six months and for an out-of-pocket incremental expenditure of no more than $15,000 to $20,000 and possibly much less, an organization should be able to develop at least one in-house TQM expert, have fairly knowledgeable primary and secondary leaders, and have a plan for training. Depending on how much donated training an organization can receive, the out-of-pocket cost could be much lower than $15,000. Corporations, many of whom are cutting their annual monetary contributions to colleges, may be able to donate a slot or two in their own in-house quality training programs. It is also important to keep the expert well trained, which means an annual expenditure of at least $3,000.

When the organization has an in-house expert and trained primary and secondary leaders, leadership must decide if it is really going to commit to moving ahead. While the next step of rolling out training to the employees entails some incremental cost, this is also the point where the institution starts to incur the soft cost associated with changing the corporate culture. If the leaders have learned their TQM lessons, they now know that they will be changing the way in which they and everyone else do their work. To move ahead without conviction and commitment is a prescription for failure. Fumbling the implementation or trying to stop the paradigm shift once it is under way will lower employee morale and reduce productivity.

Basic Cost of Training Facilitators and Group Leaders. If the senior leadership is totally committed to moving ahead, the next step is to train team facilitators and leaders. Teams dealing with complicated problems benefit from having an outside person facilitate the team meetings (Yoest, 1993). This is especially true as teams first begin to operate and the mechanics of good meetings and the use of quality tools are still new for everyone. Eventually, many teams will be able to function with either the team leader or various team members acting as facilitators. Facilitator and team leader training involves training both in group dynamics and in problem-solving processes and tools. These include such processes as developing team mission statements, brainstorming, and nominal group techniques. The training would also cover the proper use of affinity charts, Pareto charts, flowcharts, fishbone diagrams, force field analysis, control charts, and surveys. Just as individual familiarity with quality tools will range from some to none, so will familiarity with the techniques of group facilitation. This training will require at least ten to fifteen half-day sessions, and the cost of materials can range from $50 to $150 per person depending on how much is purchased. Fourteen employees at St. John Fisher College initially received this training, and it was later provided for all team leaders.

The first facilitator training course was conducted by a loaned executive (a quality facilitator trainer) from a local corporation. The in-house quality expert along with the primary and secondary leaders of the organization should become capable of leading the facilitator training. Faculty members in statistics, psychology, and marketing from one's own institution can make valuable contributions to such topics as surveying, group behavior, and focus group research. A library of audiovisual and other training materials can be acquired for between $4,000 and $8,000.

Cost of General Employee Training. The incremental cost of general employee training can be as low as the cost of materials and refreshments. The basics of group process and TQM can be covered in five half-day sessions. Materials and incidentals for five half-day training sessions will be $6.00 to $8.00 per half-day per person.

Incremental Cost of TQM. Over the past three years, the direct annual incremental cost of quality management at St. John Fisher College was one half-time clerical position plus approximately $80 per FTE administrative employee. Now that the vast majority of employees has been trained and the audiovisual training materials library has been established, the cost has dropped in the current fiscal year to $33 per FTE employee. Given that new employees need to be trained as they join the college and that refresher training needs to be available, that amount is not likely to go down soon.

Benefits of TQM

While it was easy to set up a new budget line to capture the incremental costs of TQM, the benefits have not been as easy to measure in a purely incremental fashion. However, there is a conceptual measure against which the expenditures can be judged. Since many of the improvements in quality relate to improved customer services that will help to attract or retain students, the incremental cost of TQM can be restated as a given number of students. Figure 7.1 illustrates that, in fiscal years 1992 and 1993, covering the incremen-

Figure 7.1. Cost and Benefit of TQM Measured in Dollars and Students

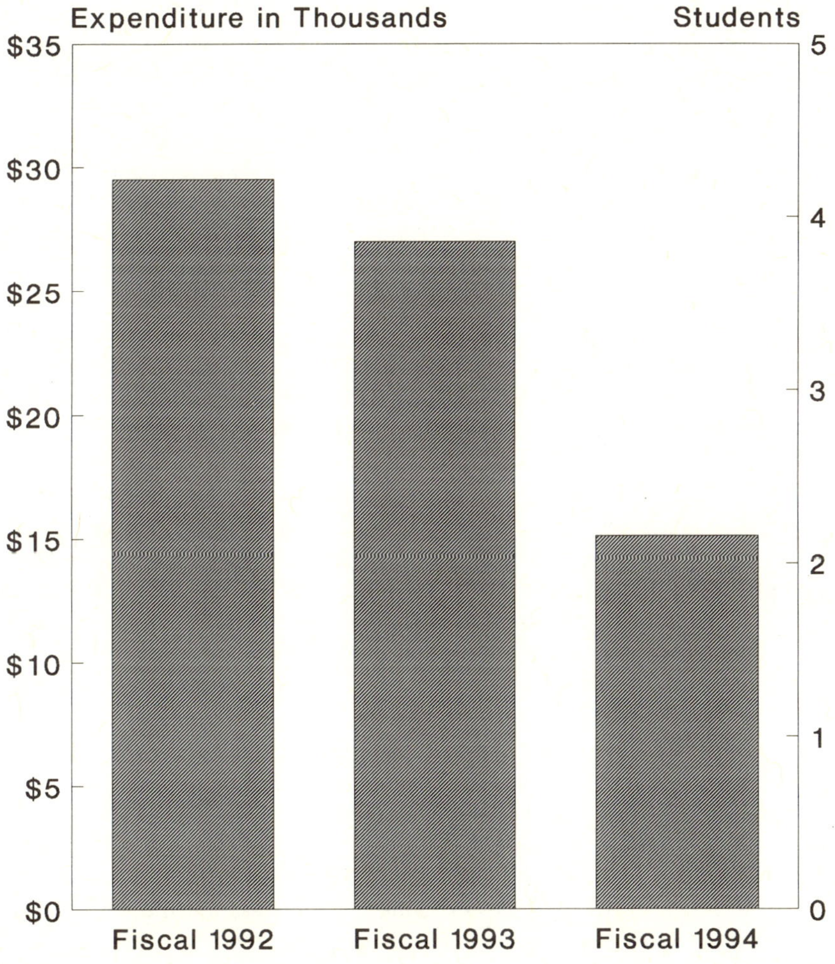

tal cost of TQM required the college to retain or enroll four students per year. Given the lower level of expenditures in the current year—fiscal year 1994—only two additional students are required. This calculation treats a student's value as equal to the tuition that he or she pays plus enrollment-related government appropriations minus the unfunded financial aid discount and the marginal cost of instruction and support services. To simplify the construction of Figure 7.1, the value of an additional student enrolled or retained was assumed to be constant over the three years that are illustrated.

The benefits of TQM at St. John Fisher College have come in a variety of forms. In general, the goals of TQM are to improve or maintain customer satisfaction while reducing costs or holding them constant. Occasionally, teams will increase customer satisfaction and reduce cost at the same time. This is most likely to happen when a team simplifies a process in which customers must participate, for example, course registration. In some cases—for example, in the mail room, computer center, and financial aid office—improvements that increased efficiency enabled teams to deal with increased workloads without adding staff. In other cases, increased efficiency has enabled teams to maintain productivity with reduced staffing. For example, the purchasing and accounts payable team was able to simplify its operations enough to eliminate 8 percent of this function's staffing. Teams have been able to find ways of dealing with reduced supply budgets while maintaining output that still meets customer expectations. For example, the payroll team at the college reduced the cost of postage by sending pay stubs through interoffice mail. Teams in every administrative area have increased customer satisfaction by making better use of existing resources.

FTE student enrollment at St. John Fisher College is approximately 6 percent higher now than it was in 1988, while administrative FTE employment has decreased slightly, and general support budgets are nominally the same. Given the wide range of external forces affecting the college, these changes in enrollment, staffing, and budget probably would have happened whether or not St. John Fisher College had adopted TQM. Nevertheless, despite the pressure that increased enrollment puts on the employees of the college, student and parent satisfaction with administrative services has increased along with administrative employee morale. (An outside marketing firm conducts an annual survey for the college.) It is hard not to believe that somewhere among those increasingly satisfied students and parents there are at least two to four who have come or stayed longer because of the treatment that they have received. With two to four incremental students, the St. John Fisher College TQM program breaks even. Beyond that, the program makes a net positive contribution to the bottom line.

Conclusion

The experience of St. John Fisher College shows that, while a good bean counter can identify the incremental costs associated with the use of TQM as the method of operating a college, the incremental benefits are difficult to pin down. In today's environment, a conservative CFO can dismiss enrollment increases and budget cuts as the inevitable consequence of external forces. But the CFO should not ignore the value of positive employee morale and increased customer satisfaction as forces that attract and retain students.

References

Brassard, M. *The Memory Jogger Plus.* Methuen, Mass.: GOAL/QPC, 1989.

Coate, L. E. "TQM on Campus: Implementing Total Quality Management in a University Setting." *NACUBO Business Officer,* 1990, *24* (5), 26–35.

Deming, W. E. *Out of the Crisis.* Cambridge, Mass.: Center for Advanced Engineering Study, Massachusetts Institute of Technology, 1982.

Doyle, M., and Straus, D. *How to Make Meetings Work.* New York: Jove Books, 1976.

Juran, J. *Juran on Leadership for Quality: An Executive Handbook.* New York: Free Press, 1989.

Mann, N. R. *The Keys to Excellence: The Story of the Deming Philosophy.* Los Angeles: Prestwick Books, 1985.

Melan, E. "Quality Improvement in Higher Education: TQM in Administrative Functions." *CUPA Journal,* 1993, *44* (1), 7–18.

Salmon, V. "Quality in American Schools." *Quality Progress,* 1993, *26* (10), 73–75.

Schargel, F. "Total Quality in Education." *Quality Progress,* 1993, *26* (10), 67–70.

Scherkenbach, W. W. *The Deming Route to Quality and Productivity.* Washington, D.C.: CEE Press, 1986.

Scholtes, P. R. *The Team Handbook.* Madison, Wis.: Joiner, 1988.

Shafer, B., and Coate, E. "Benchmarking in Higher Education." *NACUBO Business Officer,* 1992, *26* (5), 28–35.

Yoest, D. "To Train or Not to Train?" *Quality Progress,* 1993, *26* (7), 73–75.

ALAN J. NORTON is vice president for financial affairs at St. John Fisher College, Rochester, New York.

Conclusion

Some individuals might question the rationale of this sourcebook. They would argue that forty years have proved the principles and practices of TQM. Many of the nonstatistical precepts of quality management—break down the barriers between organizational units; urge customers to define quality in their own terms; empower employees to deliver customer-satisfying service—make good sense. So why bother asking the question, Is it worth doing? They would say that the only question really worth asking is, How? and add that the answer can be found in the dozens of books and articles on the subject published in the last decade. From this perspective, we have only to pay close attention to the implementation of quality management—to the process of transforming the culture. The results will take care of themselves.

I have my doubts. I do not believe that important decisions should be made on faith alone. Perhaps this is just my own secularism, but it seems to me that it is possible to have too much faith. Being absolutely sold on the value of anything can create its own false comfort.

I mention this because the impetus to produce this volume came not from my background in business or consulting work in quality but from two articles on the same opinion page of a Sunday issue of the *Los Angeles Times*. One article (Dworkin, 1993) was prompted by the highly publicized case of the Siamese twins born to a young couple in Illinois. A prenatal exam showed twin fetuses sharing one heart. The parents, who had no health insurance, decided to bring the fetuses to term and let the doctors attempt to separate the babies even though one would certainly die and the other would have only a 1 percent chance of surviving more than a few months. The quality of the life that she could live if she did survive was questionable. The total cost of the procedure might exceed a million dollars.

The author of the article believed that the choice was motivated by something he called the *rescue principle:* Our society believes that we should never give up on life if any hope remains. While the writer concedes that the principle is noble, he believes that it reflects an impossible, even absurd, ideal that we can no longer afford. He describes a simple hypothetical scenario: Suppose the couple had been people of average wealth and that they had been offered the opportunity to buy two insurance policies. The first provided that, if any of their children was born with a life-threatening defect, neonatal treatment would be covered only if it offered a reasonable (say 25 percent) chance of success. The second, much more expensive policy guaranteed such treatment no matter what the odds.

The writer contends, and I agree, that the couple might well decide that it would be better off for them and their family to buy the first policy. They could use the saved premium money to benefit their healthy children—for example, by giving them better routine medical care, or better housing, or a better education—even though they would be giving up the chance for a desperate gamble if they ever had a severely defective child. The question, of course, then becomes: Should we be willing to act as a society in a manner that was contrary to the choices that we would make if the decision were individual?

Our leaders may be operating according to this same rescue principle in their own organizations. TQM is noble. It speaks to empowerment and improvement. So the choice is a simple one: It is the right thing to do. Spend the money; make the investment. But would those same leaders be willing to make the same kind of decisions in their own lives if they knew as little about the costs and benefits? Would they write a blank check against their own checking account?

Every day, increasing numbers of companies, hospitals, and now colleges are committing themselves to something about which they know little. They do not know what it will cost them (and they have no mechanisms in place to track costs), and they do not know what results they can expect. These organizations have apparently opted for faith in the hopes that TQM will rescue them.

The second article (Lindner, 1993) examined the cost of death. California restored the death penalty in 1977. One of the driving forces was the felt need to get tough on crime. Others claimed that life imprisonment without parole cost too much. Why should we pay to keep killers alive? Nevertheless, when the death penalty was restored, Californians thought that it was important for trials to be fair and appellate review to be thorough.

The author of the article undertakes a counting exercise. It costs the taxpayer about $6,500 a day to run a courtroom, taking the salaries of judge and staff, security, overhead, depreciation, and so on into account. An average death-penalty case lasting fifty days has a baseline cost of $325,000. Next, the author adds the cost of prosecutors and investigating officers and of appeals and reviews. By the time society is in a position to administer a fatal injection, the bill has reached $3.5 to $4.5 million—five times the cost of sending the miscreant to prison for life.

The author concludes by asking two questions: Is it worth it to spend millions of dollars every week on a system that cripples the courts, fails to execute the guilty, and occasionally kills the innocent? Or should we not simply imprison these people for life and find a more sensible way of spending a billion dollars? If the price-of-life decision was based on the rescue principle, we might conclude that the cost-of-death decision is based on the revenge principle. The need to exact revenge is so overwhelming that we do not ask the difficult questions or allow the data to inform our answers.

A good deal of evidence suggests that a number of organizations are pursuing quality in the same way. Having latched onto the rhetoric, they pursue the philosophy of total quality management head down, facts aside, with the zeal and frenzy of a tent preacher.

I realize that TQM is not a life-or-death experience. Yet there is a common thread between these two articles and the topic of this sourcebook—that we need to make informed choices. We must operate our institutions with fiduciary responsibility in the same way that we would make decisions about our personal lives. We need to ask tough questions—questions that challenge assumptions, force thoughtful dialogue, and, wherever possible, generate solid data that can inform those choices.

It is only through such questioning that you will know whether TQM on your campus is worth doing.

Daniel Seymour
Editor

References

Dworkin, R. "The Price of Life: How High the Cost Before It Becomes Too High?" *Los Angeles Times,* Aug. 29, 1993, p. M1.

Lindner, C. L. "Cost of Death: A Billion Dollars and Counting." *Los Angeles Times,* Aug. 29, 1993, p. M1.

INDEX

Ordering Information

New Directions for Higher Education is a series of paperback books that provides timely information and authoritative advice about major issues and administrative problems confronting every institution. Books in the series are published quarterly in Spring, Summer, Fall, and Winter and are available for purchase by subscription and individually.

Subscriptions for 1994 cost $47.00 for individuals (a savings of 25 percent over single-copy prices) and $62.00 for institutions, agencies, and libraries. Please do not send institutional checks for personal subscriptions. Standing orders are accepted.

Single copies cost $15.95 when payment accompanies order. (California, New Jersey, New York, and Washington, D.C., residents please include appropriate sales tax.) Billed orders will be charged postage and handling.

Discounts for quantity orders are available. Please write to the address below for information.

All orders must include either the name of an individual or an official purchase order number. Please submit your order as follows:

Subscriptions: specify series and year subscription is to begin

Single copies: include individual title code (such as HE82)

Mail all orders to:

Jossey-Bass Publishers
350 Sansome Street
San Francisco, California 94104-1342

For single-copy sales outside of the United States, contact:

Maxwell Macmillan International Publishing Group
866 Third Avenue
New York, New York 10022-6221

For subscription sales outside of the United States, contact any international subscription agency or Jossey-Bass directly.

Other Titles Available in the
New Directions for Higher Education Series
Martin Kramer, Editor-in-Chief